CONSCIOUS
— CRAFTS —

POTTERY

First published in 2021 by Leaping Hare Press,
an imprint of The Quarto Group.
The Old Brewery, 6 Blundell Street
London, N7 9BH,
United Kingdom
T (0)20 7700 6700
www.QuartoKnows.com

for Laurie and Alma

Every effort has been made to trace the copyright holders of material
quoted in this book. If application is made in writing to the publisher,
any omissions will be included in future editions.

A catalogue record for this book is available from the British Library.

ISBN 978 0 7112 5743 6
Ebook ISBN 978 0 7112 5744 3

10 9 8 7 6 5 4 3 2 1

Design by Clare Barber
Illustrations by Robert Brandt
Photography by XDB Photography

Printed in China

CONSCIOUS CRAFTS

— CRAFTS —

POTTERY

20 MINDFUL MAKES TO RECONNECT HEAD, HEART & HANDS

Lucy Davidson

Leaping Hare Press

contents

introduction

I have been creating ever since I can remember and it's a large part of my life. I was brought up in a creative family and am lucky enough to have carried my love of making through into my career. I even married into a creative family! I have spent the last five years teaching craft workshops, and passing my skills on to other people and seeing what they do with them is the greatest feeling. Although I bring the same materials to each of my workshops, everyone goes away with something completely different because they add their own personal touch to the piece. This is what I hope you can do with the projects in this book. Each of the 20 makes has been designed so that you are able to take the techniques used in one project and apply them to another, allowing you to add your unique personality to your pottery pieces.

Play is vitally important to our wellbeing. Because I have grown up with making, I have noticed that if I go long periods without indulging my creativity, my mental wellbeing is affected. Even a day without my sketchbook or my materials is enough to make me snappy and agitated. I know instantly what will help with my mood – and that is making.

Creating something physical allows us to free up some mental space, especially if we are going through a particularly challenging time. I experienced this myself with the arrival of my little girl. Going from having all the time in the world to create and make whatever I liked to having absolutely no time at all, I started to really struggle. Luckily, my husband picked up on this and helped me find the time to treat myself to some crafting activities. Once I was able to make and create again, I found I was a lot calmer and had a clearer head to deal with my newfound motherhood.

Everyone today leads such busy lives. Work, social gatherings, family and all the other daily demands mean we don't spend as much time as we should being aware of our thoughts and feelings. Mindfulness is the act of taking your attention away from everything that's going on around you and focusing instead on what's within you and what's in front of you. Finding your inner calm and peace can be hard, but simple activities can help, and crafting with your hands is one of the easiest ways to switch off from the outside world and concentrate on the 'now'.

When we play with clay – whether it's air-drying clay, polymer clay or clay that needs to be fired – we can enjoy its tactile texture and immerse ourselves in the simple act of making. If you make a mistake, it's easy to simply start again. One of the great things about air-drying clay, in particular, is that it forces you to wait a certain amount of time until you can move on to the next part of the creative process. With this 'slow' crafting comes the joy of anticipation of the next stage of the project, before the relish of finally completing the piece.

In this book you will find 20 projects designed with all ages and skill levels in mind. Anyone can pick up a project and create something beautiful. Taking time out of your busy schedule to concentrate on yourself is a luxury, and so important. Leave your phone in another room, sit down somewhere peaceful and enjoy your time with some clay. My hope is that afterwards you will feel happier, calmer and more confident – all as a result from taking some time to sit quietly and reconnect with yourself.

Breathe. Step back.
Think. Then create.

clay recipes

Most of the projects in this book use air-drying clay, which you can buy in most art shops or very easily online. The projects mainly use white clay, but you can also buy air-drying clay in a terracotta colour, which we have used for the precious seaside vase (see page 140) and boho plant hanger (see page 102). A couple of projects in the book use polymer clay, which is also extremely easy to come by. This clay can be bought in many different colours, and needs to be baked in the oven rather than left to dry in the air. To enhance your mindful experience, why not also have a go at making your own clay from scratch? Here are some recipes to try:

Baking Soda and Cornflour Air-Drying Clay Recipe
makes approx. 500 g (1 lb 2 oz)

This very simple clay dries to a lovely opaque white but is more fragile. This recipe would be perfect for the coasters or the incense holder.

Ingredients
- 240ml (8½ fl oz/1½ cups) water
- 128g (4½ oz/1 cup) cornflour (cornstarch)
- 256g (9 oz/2 cups) baking soda

1 Stir all the ingredients together in a non-stick saucepan.

2 Put it on low heat, and cook for a few minutes, continuously stirring. When the mixture changes from a soft paste to a much thicker consistency, like porridge, remove from the heat.

3 Put the dough into a container and keep covered until it has cooled down. Keep the extra clay well wrapped when not using. You can store the clay in the fridge for 1–2 weeks.

Glue and Cornflour Air-Drying Porcelain Clay Recipe
makes approx. 300 g (10½ oz)

This homemade clay is a lot stronger. You can roll it out a lot thinner, which is ideal for any detail work you fancy making. A perfect recipe for the bunting or the herb markers.

Ingredients
- 128g (4½ oz/1 cup) cornflour (cornstarch)
- 128g (4½ oz/1 cup) PVA glue
- 1 tablespoon of vegetable oil
- 1 tablespoon of lemon juice, as a preservative

1 Stir all the ingredients together in a non-stick saucepan.

2 Put it on low heat, and cook for a few minutes, continuously stirring. Instead of the mixture looking like porridge (as above), it will be a lot more lumpy. That's when you should remove it from the heat. Try not to over cook the dough, as this will turn it hard and leathery.

3 Put the dough into a container and keep covered until it has cooled down. Keep the extra clay well wrapped when not using. You can store the clay in the fridge for 1–2 weeks.

tools and materials

The following items are commonly used in the projects in this book. You don't necessarily need to have every single piece of equipment listed here: odds and ends you have lying around the house can often work just as well (and the great thing about air-drying clay is that it washes off easily!).

1 Baking tray You will need a baking tray to bake your polymer pieces on. If it has any grease leftover from cooking that just won't shift, don't forget to lay a sheet of baking paper down so that the grease does not transfer onto your pieces.

2 Knitting needle A thin knitting needle or skewer can be used for making holes.

3 Clay modelling tools Clay tools are used for every project, so I recommended that you get hold of a beginner's starter pack. You can find these in most art shops or online. However, if you don't have clay tools, a kitchen utensil can often do the trick.

4 Rolling pin (wooden or plastic) Probably the most used tool in this book. Whether you use a wooden one or a plastic one is up to you; plastic ones are easier to clean (although both will clean up fine with a damp cloth). If you are buying a clay tool pack, a small rolling pin will generally be included.

5 Cling film/Plastic wrap To stop your air-drying clay from drying out, wrap it nice and tight in cling film/plastic wrap so that the air does not get to it. This will make your clay last longer.

6 Pencil with rubber on the end A pencil with a rubber on the end is the perfect tool to draw out all your patterns. If you make a mistake, it's easy to just rub it out!

7 Pliers You will need pliers if you want to add any wire to your projects. Round-nose pliers are best, but any long-nose pliers will work.

8 Cookie cutters You can get cookie cutters in all shapes and sizes, but we have used circular ones in this book. They are great for getting the perfect shape and perfect edge with not a lot of mess!

9 Newspaper or baking paper (parchment) This helps to protect your work surface from wet, sticky clay. Lay a sheet down before you start making. This is especially recommended if you are using terracotta clay, as this can stain.

10 Clear water-based varnish To protect your final pieces, paint them with a layer of varnish. This will seal any paintwork and protect the clay from getting marked.

11 Alphabet stamps If you want to add some text to your pieces but are too afraid to paint it on, alphabet stamps are a good solution. While your clay is still wet, gently press your chosen letters into the clay. Alternatively, use the stamps to apply paint to your piece once the clay is dry.

12 Old toothbrush An old toothbrush is great for paint splattering. Simply dip your toothbrush in watered-down acrylic paint, hover it over your clay piece and run your finger along the bristles. This will create a lovely speckled effect on your piece.

13 Paintbrushes A selection of paintbrushes in different sizes are used in the book. Paintbrushes with smaller heads are perfect for painting on tiny details, while larger, round-headed brushes can be used for coating on the varnish.

14 Ruler You will need a ruler to measure out lengths of clay. A metal ruler is best, as it is easier to clean.

15 Glitter Glitter is a fun way to add decoration to your polymer clay. Simply scatter some glitter onto your work surface, roll your polymer clay into the glitter, and then bake the clay as you would normally. You can also add some glitter to your varnish: mix in a sprinkling of glitter and varnish your piece as you would normally.

16 Acrylic craft paints Acrylic paint is used for quite a few of the projects in the book. You can buy it online or pick it up at your local art shop. Why not try some metallic paint to add that extra sparkle? Acrylic paint can be applied directly onto your dry clay pieces.

17 Paint pen This is a really great quick-and-easy way to add decoration to your final makes. It's completely mess free and you can keep it for another project later on.

18 Glue A strong adhesive is needed to secure any extras to your pieces, for example, brooch pins.

19 Wire We've used wire for a few projects in this book, perfect for the feather wall hanging (see page 126) and abstract earrings (see page 46). Be careful of your fingers, as the ends can be quite sharp.

20 Watercolour paints Watercolours are great for producing a 'wash' effect. You can buy them in small pocket-sized palettes, which are often found in the children's section of the art shop. Simply water them down and sweep the brush across your dried clay, making sure you don't use too much water as this will wet the clay too much.

21 Scales You can use any type of kitchen scales for measuring out your clay. Digital ones are best, as you will get a more accurate weight for any smaller pieces of clay, but don't worry too much if you don't have these.

22 Scissors A small pair of scissors comes in handy for most projects. Remember to always clean any clay or glue from the scissors after use so that it doesn't dry and ruin your scissors.

23 Fine sandpaper You will need a fine sandpaper to get rid of any rough edges that are left on the clay once it has dried. You can buy this online or at any hardware shop.

24 Tape This tape is a great addition to your toolbox, perfect for wrapping your rope ends so they don't fray. Tape it straight onto the clay so that you can paint a perfect straight line. It has many uses!

25 Fabric scissors Use your fabric scissors for trimming any fabric that you use. Never use fabric scissors on paper, or you will blunt them.

26 Scalpel or knife and cutting mat You will need a scalpel or knife to cut your clay. You can protect your work surface by using a cutting mat. Place the clay on the cutting mat, with a sheet of newspaper in between, and cut, using a ruler to create a straight, sharp line.

14

15

16

17

18

19

21

20

22

23

24

25

26

useful techniques

Handy Hints

- Wrap any unused pieces of air-drying clay in cling film (plastic wrap). This will stop the clay from drying out and allow it to be used again.
- When working with air-drying clay, keep a glass of water nearby in case you feel the clay starting to dry out. Adding a small amount of water will help moisten the clay, although try not to add too much.
- When drying air-drying clay, you may need to turn the piece over occasionally, so that it dries evenly.
- Warm polymer clay in your hands for a few minutes before using it. This will make the clay more pliable.
- Do not put your clay dishes in the dishwasher. If you need to clean them, gently dab them with a damp cloth. Don't use any soap or detergent on your pieces.

See left for a few useful tips to help you as you experiment with clay and try out the various project ideas.

Over the next few pages, you'll find some of the most common techniques used in the book. You can refer back to these detailed descriptions and step-by-step illustrations at any time if you get stuck when working on the projects.

the basics

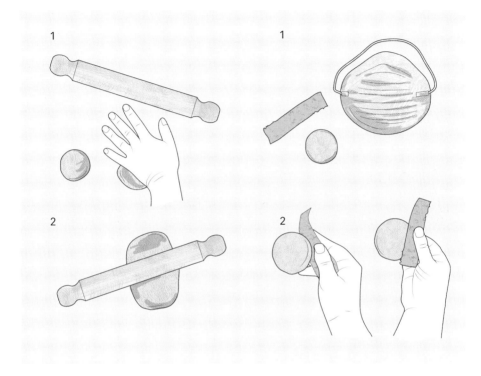

rolling out clay

1   Roll the clay into a ball between your hands. Place the ball on your work surface, then press down on it firmly with the palm of your hand to create a large coin shape. This will make the clay easier to roll out.

2   Take your rolling pin and roll the clay out.

smoothing rough edges

1   To create nice, smooth edges on your clay pieces, wait until the clay is completely dry. Tear off a small piece of fine sandpaper. Be aware that using sandpaper will create a lot of dust, so it is recommended that you put on a mask before you get started, and work outside if possible.

2   Gently rub the sandpaper along the edges and both sides of the clay. Keep gently sanding the piece until you have a nice, smooth finish. Then gently brush the clay with your finger to remove any excess dust.

making holes in clay

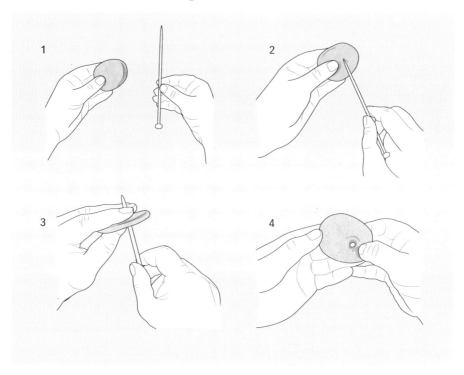

1 To make a hole in your clay, you can use either one of your clay tools or a skewer or thin knitting needle.

2 Holding the clay in one hand, gently insert the skewer through the wet clay.

3 Push the skewer out the other side between your fingers (this helps to keep the shape of your piece).

4 Smooth out any rough edges around the hole using your thumb.

merging two pieces of clay

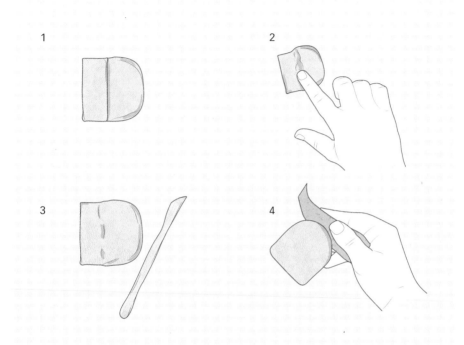

1. To create smooth, neat edges, lay the two pieces of clay on top of each other.

2. Press the top edge of the clay into the bottom piece of clay with your finger, using a swiping motion. Keep swiping with your finger until all of the edges are merged.

3. Next start to clean the clay with a flat-edged clay tool, using the same swiping motion. Keep going until the clay is completely smoothed out.

4. Once the clay is completely dry, use your sandpaper to sand down any rough patches that you missed.

joining two pieces of clay: hatching

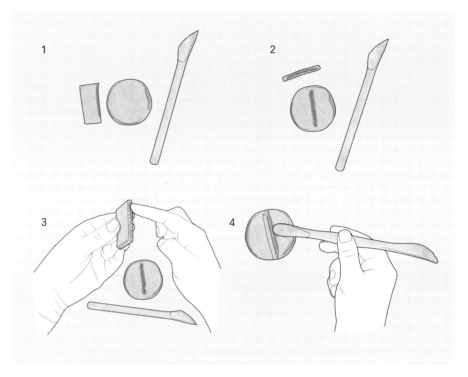

1 To hatch two pieces together, set out your clay and a sharp-ended clay tool on your work surface.

2 Use the clay tool to scratch little criss-cross patterns on both of the surfaces that you want to join.

3 Dab some water onto one of the pieces with your finger.

4 Place the two pieces together and merge the clay together on all sides, using a flat-edged clay tool.

joining two pieces of clay: worming

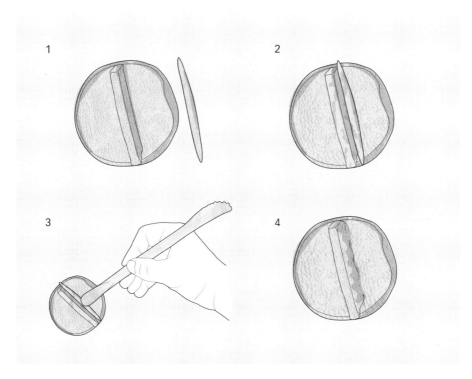

1 You can merge two pieces of clay using an extra piece of clay. Roll the extra piece of clay into a small, worm-like shape.

2 Lay the worm in the crease of the two pieces, making sure it's pushed right in.

3 Using a flat-edged clay tool, push down on the worm to merge it into the crease.

4 Keep gently pressing until the worm has merged into the sides of the clay. Leave to dry. Larger pieces that need connecting will need many worms; these can be merged section by section.

imperfect pots

Tools and materials
makes 2

To make:
- 2 x glass jars, sized 10 x 10 cm (4 x 4 inches) and 10 x 19 cm (4 x 7½ inches)
- Baking paper (parchment)
- Masking tape
- 750 g (1 lb 10 oz) white air-drying clay
- Scales
- Rolling pin
- Ruler
- Scalpel
- Clay modelling tools
- Circular cookie cutter, slightly larger than the base of your jars (optional)

To finish:
- Fine sandpaper
- Acrylic craft paints
- Small dishes (for the paints)
- Small flat acrylic paintbrush
- Clear water-based varnish
- Paintbrush for varnishing

Introduce a bit of character to your home with these imperfectly personal pots, which take inspiration from nature to bring the outside in and help you breathe a little more easily. Whether they are adding colour to your kitchen or detail to your desk space, they will give your home the human touch that everybody craves – a little bit of homemade warmth to create that cosy feeling. The smaller pot is ideal for any pencil sharpeners or rubbers you might have lying around.

These pots also make great gifts for loved ones. Who wouldn't want to receive a beautiful pot made especially for them? There's nothing quite as touching as being able to feel the hand of the maker in a personal gift.

Feel the moment and move on to the next one.

to make

1 To prevent the clay from sticking, wrap baking paper (parchment) completely around the outside of the jars and secure with masking tape.

2 Cover your work surface, and weigh out 750 g (1 lb 10 oz) of white air-drying clay.

3 Roll out the clay to roughly 5 mm (¼ inch) thick all over. The piece will need to be large enough to wrap around your largest jar.

4 Measure two strips of clay: the strip for the larger jar needs to be 25 cm (10 inches) long and 15 cm (6 inches) high; and the strip for the smaller jar needs to be 22 cm (8½ inches) long and 7 cm (2¾ inches) high. Using a ruler and scalpel, cut out the strips of clay.

5 Place your jars horizontally on top of the clay strips at the short edge. Roll each jar along the clay strip, picking the clay up as you roll, until the whole jar is covered. You will need the ends of the clay to overlap by 1 cm (½ inch). Trim off any excess clay.

6 Using your fingers or a clay modelling tool, merge the clay together to create a seam. Keep pressing and smoothing the two joins together until you have a clean join on both pots.

7 Take the leftover clay and roll out another piece of clay that is roughly 5 mm (¼ inch) thick all over. Using a cookie cutter that is slightly bigger than the base of your first jar, cut out a circle. Alternatively, you can lightly trace around the base of your jar using a scalpel and then cut out the shape, adding an extra 5 mm (¼ inch) all the way around. Repeat for the second jar.

8 Place the circles of clay on the bases of your jars and merge the seams together, using your fingers or a clay modelling tool. If you find the clay is starting to dry out, dip your fingers in water. This will help with any cracking.

9 Once you have smoothed out all your seams, leave the pots to dry for 24 hours.

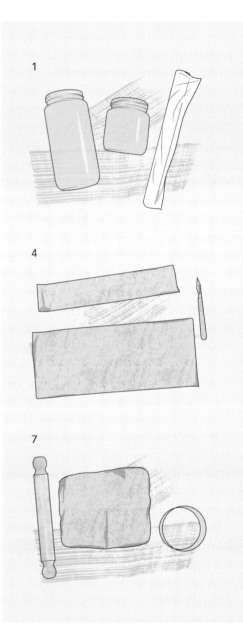

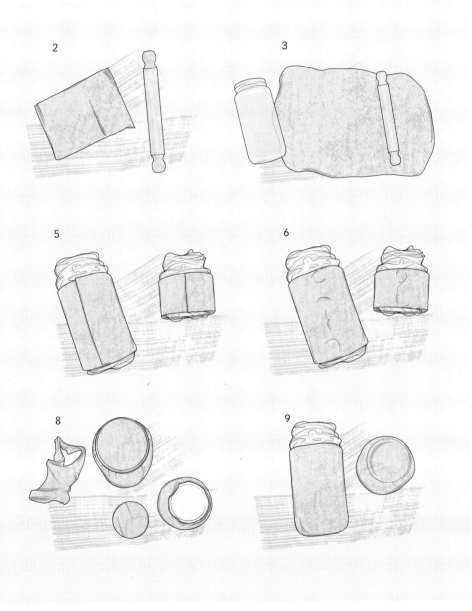

2

3

5

6

8

9

to finish

1   Once the pots are completely dry, remove the glass jars. If you have trouble with this, heat the clay gently with a hairdryer and the glass jars will slip out.

2   Using a small piece of sandpaper, sand off any rough pieces of clay.

3   Prepare your acrylic paints. Pour a small amount of each of your chosen colours into a small dish and water them down a little.

4 You are now ready to decorate your pots with abstract patterns. Be bold and experiment with colours. Start by creating simple repeat patterns at the top and bottom of the pots, then decorate the middle section. You might want to practise your patterns on a piece of paper first. When you have finished your designs, leave the pots to dry for 4 hours or until all the paint is dry.

5 Once both pots are dry, cover them in a coat of clear varnish. Leave to dry for 24 hours before using them.

nana's vintage lace coasters

Tools and materials

makes 6

To make:

- 250 g (9 oz) white air-drying clay
- Scales
- Rolling pin
- Lace in various patterns
- Circular 8 cm (3 inch) cookie cutter

To finish:

- Fine sandpaper
- Your choice of watercolour paints
- Thick, round watercolour paintbrush
- Clear water-based varnish
- Paintbrush for varnishing

Has your Nana kindly passed down her beloved vintage lace tablecloth or placemats and you are not sure what to do with them? If they are not to your taste but you can't bear to get rid of them, this project allows you to reuse them to create something beautiful for your home that you will be proud to show off. Don't worry if you don't have any vintage lace; you can often find a great selection of offcuts in the 'bargain bin' at your fabric store, or you can try your local second-hand shop. If you have a few different pieces of lace, this will allow you to create different patterns on your coasters. Once you have used the lace, you will just need to wash it and it will be as good as new.

Matching placemats make a great addition to these lace coasters. You can use exactly the same method to make them, but instead of using cookie cutters to create the coaster shapes, trace around a large plate or dish. You will have the perfect dinner set to show off to your friends and make your Nana proud!

to make

1 Cover your work surface. To make six coasters you will need to weigh out 250g (9 oz) of white air-drying clay. Using your rolling pin, roll the clay out until it is around 1 cm (½ inch) thick all over, smoothing out any creases that appear.

2 Lay your lace on the rolled-out clay. If you have a few different pieces of lace, play around with the placement, and layer different pieces on top of one another to create different abstract textures and patterns.

3 When you are happy with the placement of the lace, roll the rolling pin over the top, applying medium pressure to ensure that the lace imprints onto the clay. The clay will get thinner, but make sure it remains at least 5 mm (¼ inch) thick.

4 Cut out three coasters using your cookie cutter, keeping in mind where you would like the pattern to appear.

5 Roll the leftover clay into a ball and repeat steps 1–4 to make three more coasters. You will notice that the clay will become a little dry, so try not to overwork it or it will start to crack.

6 Before your coasters dry out, dip your finger in some water and run it around the edges of the coasters to smooth out any rough edges. Put the coasters aside and leave them to dry for 2 days, turning them over halfway so that they dry evenly.

Make art to settle your mind.

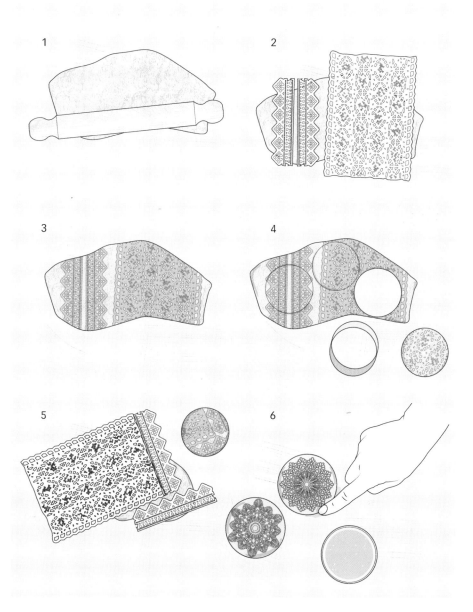

1

2

3

4

5

6

to finish

1 When your coasters are completely dry and
   hard, it's time to decorate. If any sharp edges
   remain, sand them off with a small piece of
   fine sandpaper.

2 Prepare your chosen watercolours; make sure
   your paint is quite watery, like a 'wash'.

3 Load your paintbrush with the watered-down paint and sweep it across the top of your first coaster in wide strokes, applying a light pressure. Be careful not to apply too much paint – you don't want too much water to soak into your air-dried clay or it will become wet and brittle. Repeat for the remaining coasters; you can either make them all the same or use a different colour for each one.

4 Leave to dry for 4 hours. If you would like the paint colour to be darker, apply a second coat.

5 Once the paint is dry and you are happy with the colour, apply a layer of clear varnish to the top and sides of your coasters, using a different brush. This will seal and protect your coasters from any spills. Leave to dry for 24 hours.

marbled jewellery dish

Tools and materials
makes 1

To make:
- 25 g (1 oz) peach polymer clay
- 25 g (1 oz) lemon polymer clay
- 25 g (1 oz) pale pink polymer clay
- Scales
- Plastic rolling pin
- Round enamel bowl, 13 cm (5 inches) in diameter
- Scalpel
- Baking tray

To finish:
- Gold acrylic craft paint or gold nail varnish
- Small dish (for the paint)
- Small acrylic paintbrush
- Clear water-based varnish
- Medium-sized paintbrush for varnishing

Marbling is one of my favourite techniques to experiment with when creating with polymer clay. It's so satisfying, and I love to see the patterns taking shape as I go – you never really know where it will lead.

This dish uses a calm and complementary colour palette, but there is nothing stopping you from using bright and bold primary colours if they are more to your taste. Alternatively, you could choose colours that complement your home interior. The dish also makes a lovely gift for a colour-loving friend.

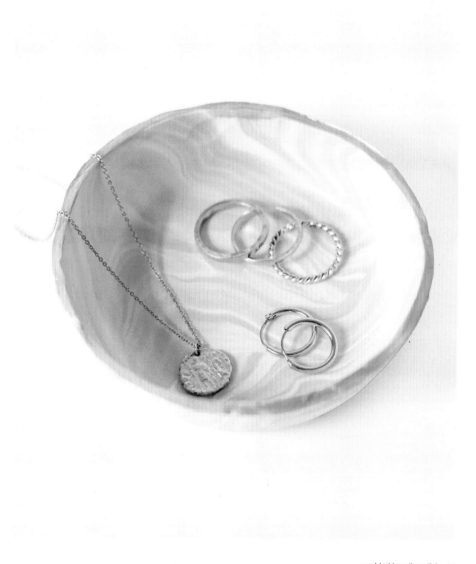

to make

1 Preheat your oven to 135°C (275°F/Gas Mark 1). Cover your work surface and weigh out 25g (1 oz) of polymer clay in each of the three colours. To marble the clay, start by rolling each block of clay between your hands into a snake-like shape measuring 20 cm (8 inches). This will take a few minutes, as you will need the clay to warm up before it becomes pliable.

2 Once all three are the same shape, lay them on top of each other. Twist the three coloured snakes together.

3 Using your hands, roll the twisted pieces of clay into another long snake shape, then fold it in half and twist again. Repeat this step four times, finishing by rolling out the clay into a long snake. You will notice the clay has started to marble.

4 To create some nice curves in your marble pattern, lay out your snake into a zigzag, then roll it out again.

5 Next lay your snake into a spiral pattern, then place the clay in between your hands and roll it into a ball. This will create some lovely unique patterns in your piece of clay.

6 With your rolling pin, roll your ball of clay into a flat circle that measures 17 x 17 cm (6½ x 6½ inches) and is 5 mm (¼ inch) thick all over.

Trust your process.

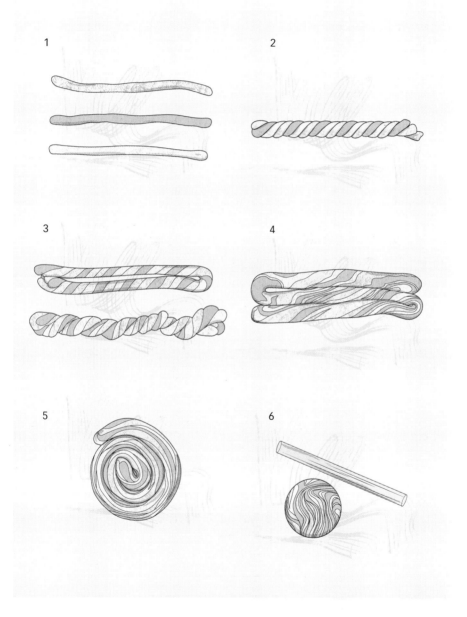

1

2

3

4

5

6

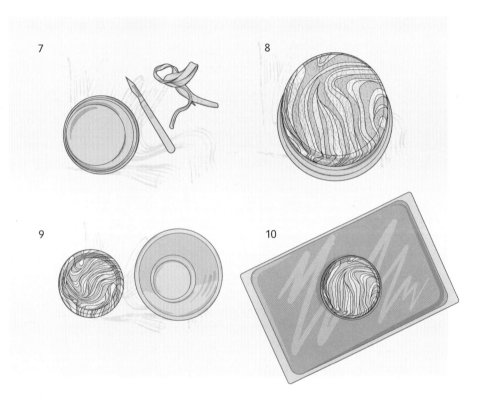

7 Lay your enamel dish upside down on the clay circle. Run a sharp scalpel around the bottom of the dish to trim off any excess clay.

8 Remove the trimmed clay circle and place it over the base of the enamel dish. Using your hands, gently press the clay down to form the shape of the dish.

9 Leaving the clay on the base of the dish, put the dish on a baking tray and place this on the middle shelf of your preheated oven. Bake for 10 minutes.

10 After 10 minutes, remove the dish and leave it to cool for 1 hour. Then remove the clay dish from the enamel dish.

to finish

1 Once your dish has cooled, it can be decorated.
   Pour a pea-sized amount of gold acrylic craft
   paint into a dish.

2 With a clean, thin paintbrush, carefully paint
   the rim of your dish. Take your time over this
   step. If you don't have any gold acrylic paint,
   you can use a gold nail varnish instead.
   Leave to dry for 4 hours.

3 Once the gold paint is dry, coat the sides and
   inside of your dish with a layer of clear varnish,
   using a medium-sized clean paintbrush. Leave
   to dry for 12 hours, then turn over and coat the
   base. Leave to dry for another 12 hours.

wild necklace beads

Tools and materials
makes 12

To make:
- 25 g (1 oz) peach polymer clay
- 25 g (1 oz) mint green polymer clay
- 25 g (1 oz) yellow polymer clay
- 25 g (1 oz) light green polymer clay
- 25 g (1 oz) white polymer clay
- Scales
- Knife
- Skewer
- Gold glitter
- Baking paper (parchment)
- Baking tray

To finish:
- Clear water-based varnish
- Medium-sized paintbrush for varnishing
- Necklace chain
- Pliers

I love using polymer clay to create beads – they're so smooth and tactile, you won't be able to stop touching them! This beautiful necklace combines various techniques to create a set of unique designs. You can keep it simple with plain clay beads, or jazz it up by adding glitter or combining coloured clays to create a marbled effect.

Bead-making really allows you to experiment and indulge your creativity. Why not make extra-large beads for that statement piece of costume jewellery, or go small to add some subtle colour inflections to your everyday outfits?

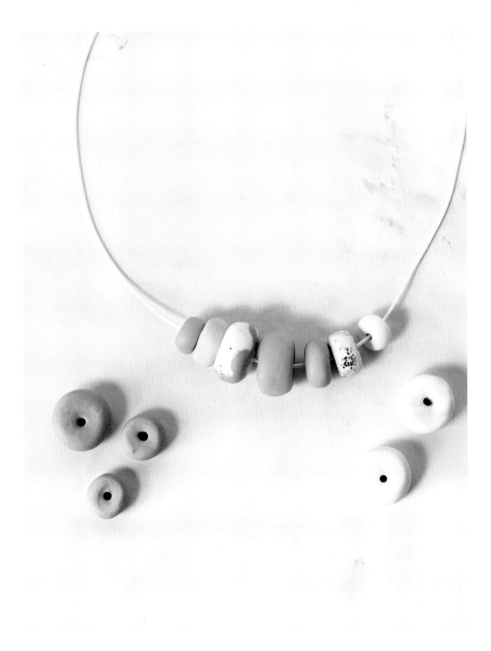

to make

1 Preheat your oven to 135°C (275°F/Gas Mark 1). Cover your work surface, and weigh out 25 g (1 oz) of polymer clay in each of the five colours.

2 With your knife, cut the peach polymer clay in half. Cut one of the pieces in half again, so that you have three pieces of clay. Put one of the smaller pieces to one side to use later.

3 Roll the large piece of clay into a ball between your hands. Do the same with the smaller piece of clay. Then press each ball between your fingers to create two slightly squashed beads.

4 With a skewer, make a hole through the middle of each bead big enough for the necklace chain to pass through.

5 Sprinkle some gold glitter on a clean surface and roll the smaller bead through the glitter. Repeat steps 1–4 for the mint green, yellow and light green polymer clays, adding glitter to some of the smaller beads if wanted.

6 With your knife, cut the white polymer clay in half, and then cut each piece in half again, so that you have four pieces of clay. Roll one piece of the white clay between your hands to create a small snake measuring about 10 cm (4 inches). Create another snake in the same way, using the piece of peach clay that you set aside in step 2.

Find a quiet corner, clear a space and gather your tools ready to create.

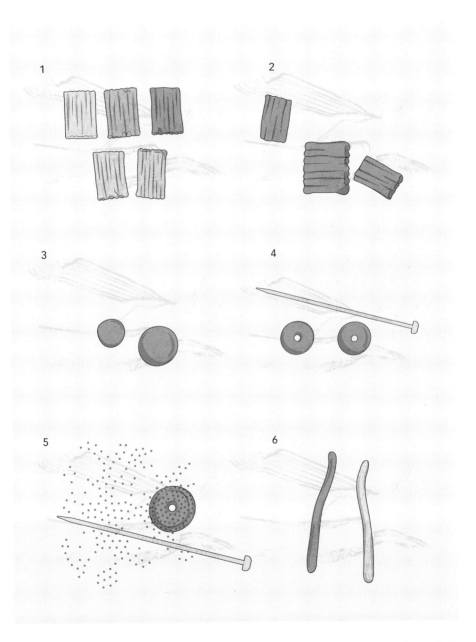

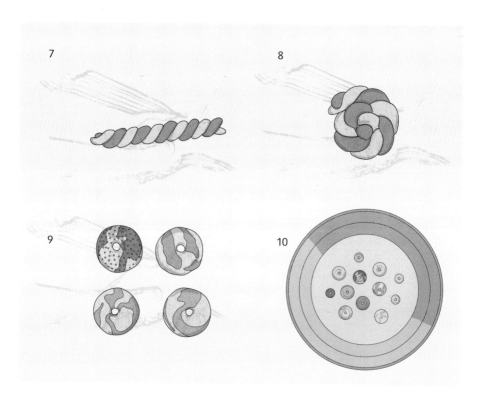

7 Twist your two snakes together. You can make
   the twists as tight or as loose as you like –
   the tighter the twists, the more stripy the
   clay will be.

8 Roll your twisted snake out in a spiral shape,
   then place the clay in between your hands
   and roll it into a ball. This will create a
   marbled effect.

9 Gently press the ball of clay between your fingers
   to create a slightly squashed bead shape, and
   make a hole in the middle of the bead using a
   skewer. Repeat steps 4–8 with the remaining
   pieces of white, mint green, yellow and light
   green polymer clay. Add glitter if desired.

10 Once you have made all your beads, they are
   ready to go in the oven. You will need to bake
   the smaller beads for 8 minutes and the larger
   beads for 10 minutes. Place them on a baking
   tray lined with baking paper (parchment) and
   place this on the middle shelf of your preheated
   oven. Once you have taken your beads out of
   the oven, leave them to cool for 1 hour.

to finish

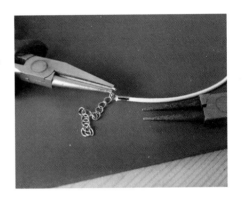

1 Once your beads are cool, coat one side of the beads with a layer of clear varnish, using a clean, medium-sized paintbrush. Leave them to dry for 12 hours, then turn over and coat the other side. Leave to dry for another 12 hours.

2 Once the beads are dry, you can create your necklace. If the holes in any of your beads are too small for the necklace chain fixings to fit through, remove the necklace fixings with pliers.

3 Thread the beads on and reattach the fixings back on to the chain.

abstract earrings

Tools and materials
makes 1 pair

To make:
- 3 g (¹/₁₀ oz) khaki green polymer clay
- 6 g (¼ oz) white polymer clay
- 12 g (½ oz) rust polymer clay
- Scales
- Skewer
- Plastic rolling pin
- Baking paper (parchment)
- Baking tray

To finish:
- Clear water-based varnish
- Small paintbrush for varnishing
- 10 cm (4 inches) gold wire
- Earring hooks

The charm of these earrings is that they have a lovely handmade feel to them, and the shapes are all slightly different – so don't worry too much if your earrings are not identical. Feel free to improvise and experiment with your own designs if you are feeling inspired.

If you are making these bold and exciting earrings for a special occasion such as a friend's wedding, you could glitz them up by adding a touch of gold leaf or try making them in complementary colours to match your outfit. You can guarantee that no one else will be wearing the same pair of statement earrings as you!

You can buy earring hooks at your local craft shop or online.

to make

1 Preheat your oven to 135°C (275°F/Gas Mark 1). Cover your work surface, and weigh out your polymer clay in each of the three colours. Cut the white clay in half so that you have two pieces.

2 Roll one of the pieces of khaki clay between your hands to create a small snake measuring about 10 cm (4 inches). Create another snake in the same way using one of your pieces of white clay.

3 Twist the two snakes together tightly, and roll them between your hands to make a long snake. This will create a marbled effect.

4 Fold the long snake in half. Then twist the two halves together, and roll the twisted clay between your hands to create a longer snake. Repeat this step a couple more times.

5 Lay your twisted snake out in a spiral shape, then place the clay in between your hands and roll it into a ball.

6 Cut the ball of clay in half. Then roll the two smaller pieces into balls.

Smile to yourself.

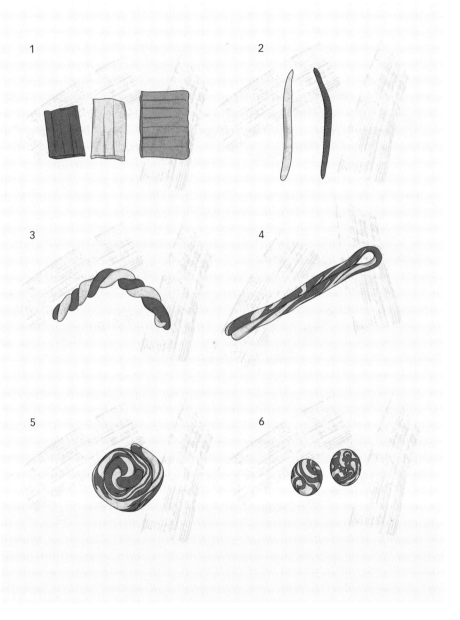

1

2

3

4

5

6

7 Using your fingers, flatten the two marbled balls to create two small discs. These will be the top part of your earrings. With a skewer, make a small hole at the top of each disc.

8 Roll the remaining white polymer clay into two small balls. Using your fingers, flatten each ball to create two small white discs. With a skewer, pierce a hole at the top of each disc, but not too close to the edge or it could break.

9 To create the bottom half of your earrings, roll the rust polymer clay into a long snake measuring 14 cm (5½ inches). Cut it in half so you are left with two snakes measuring 7 cm (2¾ inches).

10 Bend each snake into a U-shape.

11 Lay a clean piece of baking paper (parchment) over the top of your U-shaped pieces of clay, then roll your rolling pin over the top to flatten out the pieces of clay. With your skewer, pierce a hole at the top of each shape.

12 Put all the pieces on a baking tray lined with baking paper (parchment) and place this on the middle shelf of your preheated oven. Bake for 5 minutes, then remove from oven and leave to cool for 1 hour.

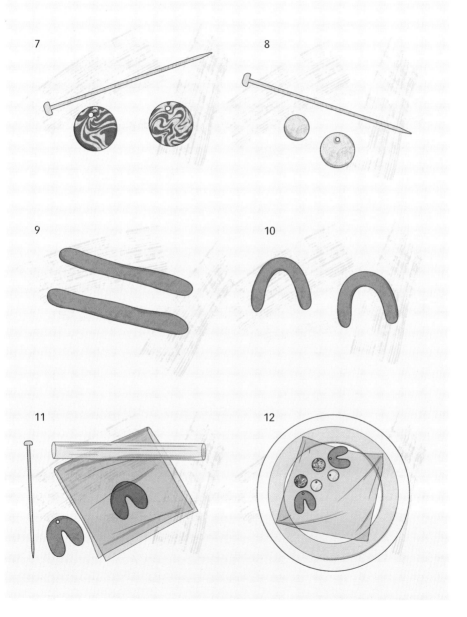

to finish

1 Once the pieces of clay are cool, coat one side with a layer of clear varnish, using a small, clean paintbrush. Leave to dry for 12 hours, then turn over and coat the other side. Leave to dry for another 12 hours.

2 Once your pieces of clay are dry, you can assemble your earrings. Stack the earring pieces together: khaki on top of rust, white on top of khaki, lining up the holes.

3 Cut 10 cm (4 inches) of gold wire, thread it through the holes, then thread it onto the earring hooks.

4 Bring the wires to the back, twist them together and cut off the excess.

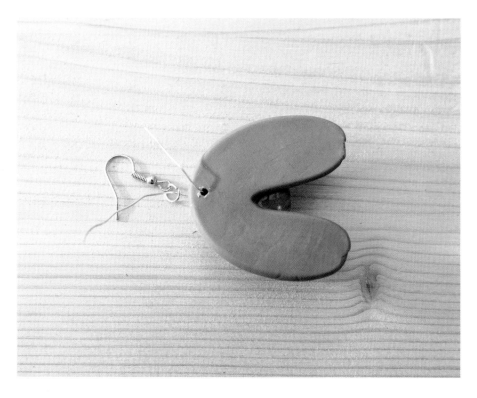

modern terrazzo-style bracelet

Tools and materials
makes 1

To make:
- 50 g (2 oz) white polymer clay
- 5 g (³⁄₁₆ oz) sand polymer clay
- 5 g (³⁄₁₆ oz) mink pink polymer clay
- 5 g (³⁄₁₆ oz) dusky pink polymer clay
- 5 g (³⁄₁₆ oz) mint polymer clay
- Scales
- Plastic rolling pin
- Scalpel
- Ruler
- Baking paper (parchment)
- Clean, empty tin can
- Baking tray

To finish:
- Clear water-based varnish
- Medium-sized paintbrush for varnishing

Terrazzo is usually made from a combination of marble, quartz and granite chips and is most commonly used on kitchen work surfaces or in tiles. Recently it's taken on a life of its own and is popping up in all the interior magazines and blogs. I love its clean look, and this project is a great way to bring the style of terrazzo into your everyday fashion. We've used a neutral colour palette to make our bracelet, but if you prefer you can choose colours that really speak to you and express your unique personality.

The repetitive task of placing individual coloured shapes to create your original terrazzo pattern is very satisfying, very similar to putting together a jigsaw puzzle. Take your time finding pieces that fit perfectly next to each other. There are no right or wrong answers – your instinct will guide you through.

to make

1. Preheat your oven to 135°C (275°F/Gas Mark 1). Cover your work surface, and weigh out your clay.

2. With your plastic rolling pin, roll out your white clay so that it measures roughly 21 x 10 cm (8 x 4 inches). The clay should be 5 mm (¼ inch) thick all over.

3. Using your hands, roll the four coloured pieces of clay into small balls. Make sure you have worked the clay well, so that it's nice and pliable.

4. With your rolling pin, roll out each piece of coloured clay so it is around 2 mm (⅛ inch) thick.

5. Using your scalpel, cut the coloured pieces of clay into lots of smaller pieces. You don't need to be too neat – you want your pieces to be lots of different shapes and sizes.

6. Start placing the small pieces of coloured clay on top of the rolled-out white clay, until it is completely covered. The pieces can be placed randomly, but try to get an even distribution of all four colours.

Find peace and calm in simple things.

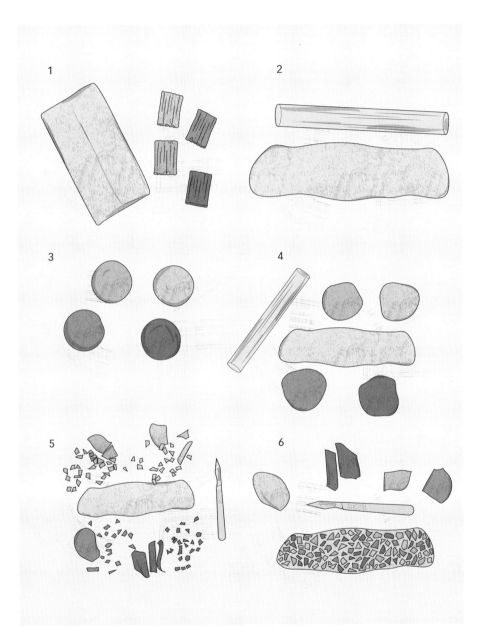

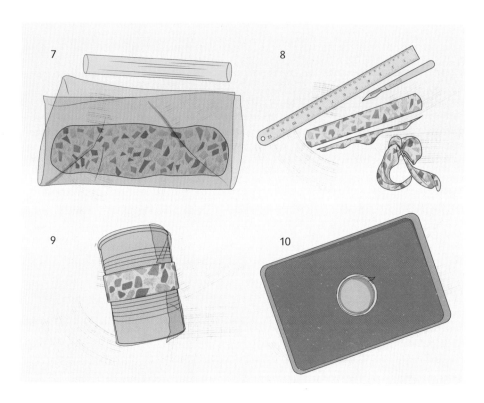

7 Once you are happy with the placement of the small pieces, lay a sheet of baking paper (parchment) over the clay, then roll a rolling pin over it a couple of times, applying a light pressure – enough to merge the coloured clays into the white clay, without flattening the white clay itself. The baking paper (parchment) will stop the rolling pin from sticking to your clay and moving the smaller pieces.

8 Using a ruler and scalpel, cut out your bracelet strip. It will need to measure 21 x 3 cm (8 x 1 inches). Round off the corners.

9 Before baking your bracelet, you will need to wrap it around a clean, empty tin can. Cover the can with baking paper (parchment), then gently wrap your bracelet around it; there will be a small gap between the two ends of the bracelet.

10 Stand the can upright on a baking tray and place it on the middle shelf of your preheated oven. Bake for 10 minutes, then remove from oven. Leave the bracelet to cool on the tin for 1 hour, then carefully slide it off the tin.

to finish

1 To protect your bracelet from everyday dirt and grease, coat it all over with a layer of clear varnish, using a clean, medium-sized paintbrush. Leave to dry for 12 hours.

2 Apply a second coat of varnish, and leave the bracelet to dry for another 12 hours. Once it is completely dry, your bracelet is ready to wear!

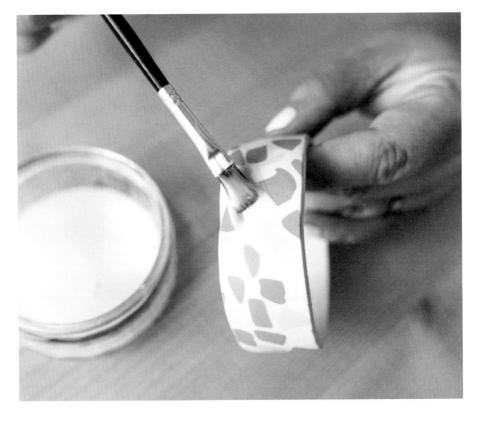

beautiful bird brooches

Tools and materials
makes 3

To make:
- 100 g (4 oz) white air-drying clay
- Scales
- Rolling pin
- Clay modelling tools
- Scalpel

To finish:
- Fine sandpaper
- Acrylic craft paints
- Small dishes (for the paints)
- Medium and small acrylic paintbrushes
- Clear water-based varnish
- Medium-sized paintbrush for varnishing
- 3 brooch backs
- Superglue

Super sweet and yet so simple, these beautiful handmade bird brooches are the perfect accessory to adorn your favourite outfit – wear one little bird for a subtle flourish or have all three flying across your lapel for a statement accessory. You can leave the brooches plain for a simple, elegant look or paint them to add a little character.

You can create any animal or flower you like for your brooches, but I chose birds because I love the freedom they represent.

The brooch backs can be bought online or at your local craft shop.

to make

1 Cover your work surface, and weigh out 100 g (4 oz) of white air-drying clay. This will be enough to make three bird brooches, each measuring approximately 6 x 6 cm (2½ x 2½ inches).

2 With your rolling pin, roll out your piece of clay so that it is around 20 x 9 cm (8 x 3½ inches) in size and 1 cm (½ inch) thick.

3 Using one of your clay modelling tools, sketch out the outline of your bird brooches. If you make a mistake, simply rub your finger over the clay and start again.

4 Once you are happy with the shapes of your birds, cut them out using a scalpel. Smooth out any rough edges using a dab of water and your finger.

5 Add features and decoration to your birds, using various clay modelling tools. These tools usually come with different-shaped ends – test out the marks they make on some leftover clay. Gently apply medium pressure and press your tool into the clay to create your marks and patterns.

6 Leave your brooches to dry for 24 hours, turning them over halfway so that the clay dries evenly.

Hold on to your good feelings.

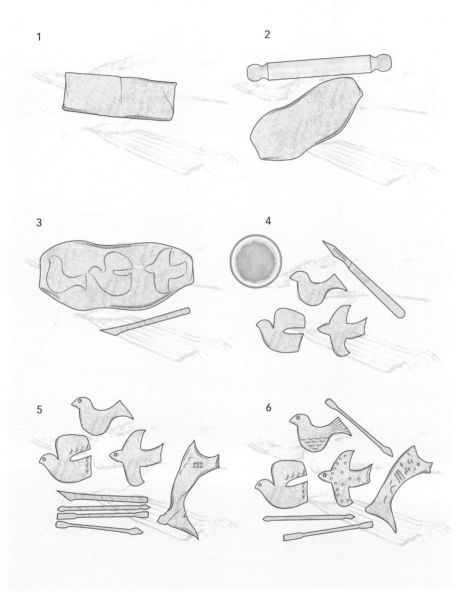

1

2

3

4

5

6

to finish

1 Once your brooches are completely dry, sand off any rough edges using fine sandpaper.

2 You can either leave your brooches plain, or you can add extra detail by painting them using acrylic paints. If you are painting them, pour a small amount of each of your chosen colours into small dishes and water them down a little to create a 'wash'.

3 Start by painting on the lighter colours with a medium brush; add the darker details afterwards with a small brush. To avoid your colours bleeding, wait 4 hours for each layer of paint to dry completely, before starting on the next.

4 Once you are happy with your decoration and the brooches are completely dry, apply a coat of clear varnish, using a clean, medium-sized paintbrush. Leave to dry for 24 hours.

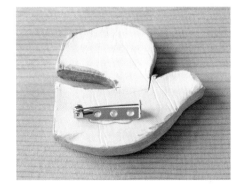

5 When your brooches are dry, glue the brooch backs onto the back of the brooches. Leave the glue to dry for 48 hours.

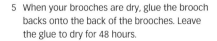

pinch pot
tealight holders

Tools and materials
makes 2

To make:
- 400 g (14 oz) white air-drying clay
- Scales
- Cling film (plastic wrap)
- Scissors
- Knitting needle
- Clay modelling tools

To finish:
- Fine sandpaper
- Acrylic craft paints
- Small dishes (for the paints)
- Large and small acrylic paintbrushes
- Clear water-based varnish
- Medium paintbrush for varnishing

Peaceful lighting is key when setting the tone for an evening of self-care. Picture taking a bath surrounded by the warm glow of candles dancing in your newly made tealight holders, perhaps indulging in your favourite book or podcast – the perfect way to escape the busyness of everyday life and create your own contemplative bubble.

The repetitive process of patterned mark-making is, by its very nature, calming and therapeutic – an ideal task to focus a busy mind. You don't even need to own any specialist clay tools; you can use anything around the house to make your marks – why not try keys or the end of a spoon? You will be surprised by how the most unlikely of domestic objects can create interesting and unique patterns.

to make

1   Cover your work surface, and weigh out 400 g (14 oz) of clay. This will be enough to make two tealight holders. Cut the clay in half, then wrap one half in cling film (plastic wrap) and leave to one side to use later.

2   Roll the other half of the clay into a ball using your hands. Try not to work the clay too much, as this will dry it out and cracks will appear.

3   Poke your thumb unto the middle of the ball of clay, stopping about two-thirds of the way down.

4   Holding the pot in the palm of your hand, start to enlarge the hole in the middle by gently pressing the sides of the clay between your thumb and two fingers. Work your way around the hole, turning the pot as you work, so that you get an even thickness of clay wall all the way around the pot. Keep enlarging the hole until the sides of your pot are 5 mm–1 cm (¼ – ½ inch) thick.

5   Place the pot on the table and gently press down on the base to flatten it. This will stop your pot from wobbling or toppling over.

6   If the rim of the pot is slightly uneven and wonky, you can trim it with a sharp pair of scissors. Smooth out any rough edges using a dab of water and your finger.

Feel the moment, breathe, then move on to the next one.

1

2

3

4

5

6

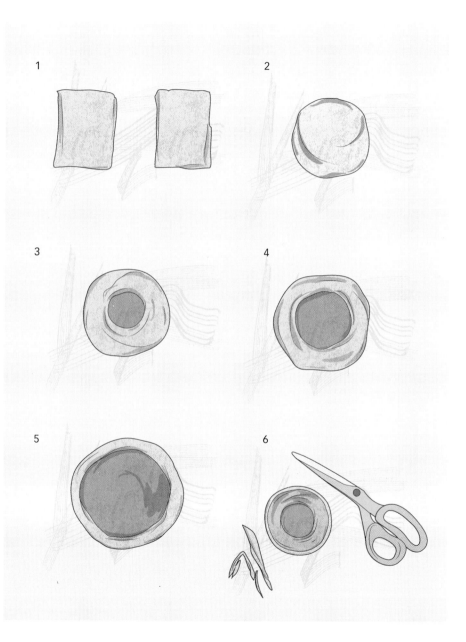

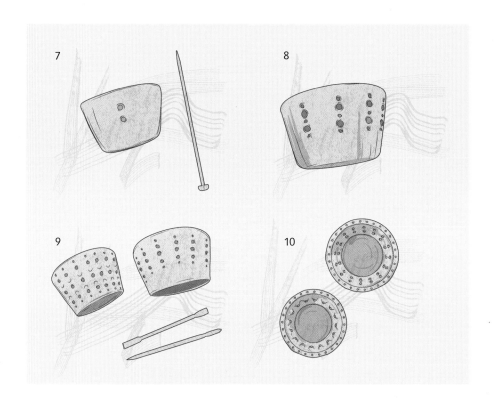

7 In order for the light from the tealights to shine through the holder, you will need to make a number of holes around the sides of your pot. To create these, pierce through the clay with a knitting needle, holding the inside of the pot with your other hand so that it doesn't collapse under the pressure.

8 Once you have made holes all the way around the pot, you can use the different-shaped ends of your clay modelling tools to add extra decoration.

9 Using the clay you set aside in step 1, repeat steps 2–8 to make your second pot.

10 Leave the two pots to dry for 24 hours, turning them upside down after 12 hours so that the bases can dry.

to finish

1 Once your pots are dry, smooth any rough edges using fine sandpaper. You are now ready to decorate your tealight holders using acrylic craft paint.

2 Using a medium-sized paintbrush, paint a wash of base colour, and allow to dry for 4 hours. Paint finer details with darker colours using a smaller paintbrush, and leave for another 4 hours.

3 Once the paint is completely dry, use a clean medium-sized paintbrush to coat your tealight holders with a layer of clear varnish. Leave to dry for 24 hours before using.

geometric light pull

Tools and materials
makes 1

To make:
- 500 g (1 lb 2 oz) white air-drying clay
- Scalpel or sharp knife
- Metal ruler
- Knitting needle or skewer

To finish:
- Fine sandpaper
- Acrylic craft paints
- Small dishes (for the paints)
- Paintbrushes in various sizes
- Newspaper or baking paper (parchment)
- Clear varnish
- 5 wooden beads
- Masking tape
- 2 m (6½ foot) of cord or thin rope, 3 mm (⅛ inch) thick

A light pull doesn't just have to be a light pull – the simplest of everyday items can bring us joy. With its combination of clay and wooden beads and its beautiful earthy tones, this light pull will give your room the uplift you are looking for. It's very simple to make, so it's perfect for when you just need to switch off. You can create as many beads as you desire, and decorate as much or as little as you please.

to make

1 First, cover your work surface. Then cut your white air-dry clay into cubes – three small, two medium and two large. Roll the three smaller cubes between your hands to create small round balls. Squash one of these down to create a small disc shape.

2 To create the ring, use your hands to roll out one of the large cubes of clay into a sausage shape approximately 20 cm (8 inches) long. Bring the two ends together and join them using your fingers.

3 To create the half-moon beads, roll the other large cube of clay between your hands to create a ball. Use a metal ruler and a scalpel or a sharp knife to cut it in half, then smooth off any rough edges with a dab of water. The half-moons might lose their shape slightly when you cut the ball of clay; if they do, gently press them back into shape with your fingers.

4 Now take your two medium-sized cubes of clay. Roll one between your hands to create a ball. Leave the other as a cube shape. Smooth off any rough edges with a dab of water.

5 Once you have made all your beads, pierce a hole through each one with a thin knitting needle or skewer. Make sure each hole is large enough for the cord to pass through it easily.

6 Once you have pierced the holes through the beads, leave them to dry for 5 days. Don't forget to turn the beads occasionally so that the clay dries evenly.

Slow down; create and breathe.

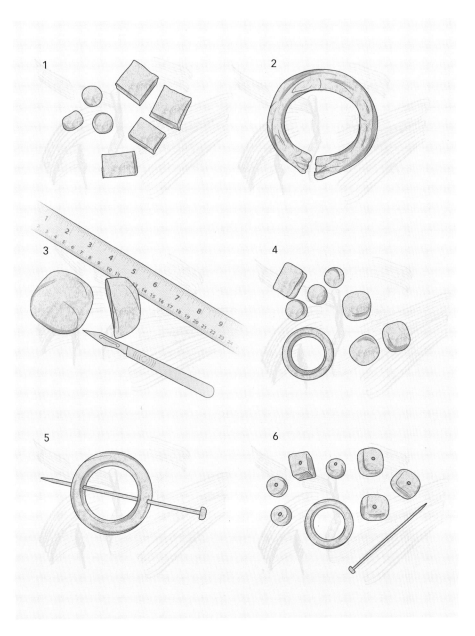

to finish

1 Once the beads are dry, sand any rough edges.

2 Pour your chosen acrylic paints into small
   dishes and paint your beads in plain colours.
   If you place the beads on the end of a paintbrush
   or skewer before painting, this will help to give
   a nice, even coating and minimize mess. Leave
   the beads to dry for 4 hours.

3 Once the large circular bead is dry, cover
   your work surface with newspaper or baking
   paper (parchment) and place the bead onto
   it. Splatter it with a darker shade of paint.
   To create this effect, use a stiffer paintbrush
   and flick the end of the brush with your
   finger. Leave to dry for 4 hours.

4   Once all the beads are dry, coat them with a clear varnish using a clean paintbrush. Varnishing will protect your light pull from grubby hands and everyday use. Leave to dry for 24 hours.

5   Once you are ready to assemble your light pull, lay the beads out in the order that you want. Add in ready-made wooden beads top and bottom. Take your cord and tie a large knot at one end, then wrap the other end of the cord in masking tape and pinch to a point to make the beads easier to thread. Thread on all your beads.

Matisse-inspired incense holder

Tools and materials
makes 1

To make:
- 250 g (9 oz) white air-drying clay
- Scales
- Rolling pin
- Metal ruler
- Scalpel
- Clay modelling tools
- Scissors
- Small piece of wire

To finish:
- Fine sandpaper
- Black acrylic craft paint
- Small dish (for the paint)
- Old toothbrush
- Newspaper or baking paper (parchment)
- Clear water-based varnish
- Paintbrush for varnishing

Get meditative with Matisse! Known for his sumptuous forms and deep calming tones, Matisse sets the perfect mood for some reflective relaxation. This incense holder, inspired by the artist, is an ideal make for art lovers.

The project gives you the opportunity to really let your creativity loose while crafting some expressive forms. The decoration of the piece involves making your own version of the popular speckle glaze, using just some paint and an old toothbrush. So simple and yet so pleasing, this make rewards your efforts from start to finish.

Focus on your breathing, be aware of your body and relax.

to make

1 First, cover your work surface. Weigh out approximately 250 g (9 oz) of white air-drying clay, and roll it out so that it is roughly 1 cm (½ inch) thick all over.

2 Using your ruler and scalpel, cut out a rectangle measuring 13 x 9 cm (5 x 3½ inches). Clean the rough edges of the rectangle using your finger and a dab of water.

3 You now need to add shapes to your base. Take the clay that is left over from step 2, and roll it out so that it is 5 mm (¼ inch) thick. Using the scalpel, lightly draw the outline of your two shapes and then carefully cut them out. Clean any rough edges with your fingers and a dab of water.

4 Before you attach your pieces to the base, make sure they fit, and you are happy with the placement. To attach your first piece, first score the underside of it, making small criss-cross lines with the sharp end of your modelling tool. Then score the area of the base where the piece will be attached. Moisten your finger and run it along the criss-cross lines on both pieces of clay, then stick the two pieces of clay together. With the softer end of your modelling tool, gently merge the two pieces of clay together, closing the seal. Attach the second piece in the same way.

5 To make the circular holder for the incense stick, roll a small piece of clay into a ball, then attach it to the base using the method described in step 4.

6 Use a small piece of wire to make a hole in the circular incense stick holder. Check that the hole is big enough to hold an incense stick before you let the clay dry. Leave to dry for 24 hours, making sure you turn your piece over halfway through so that the clay dries evenly.

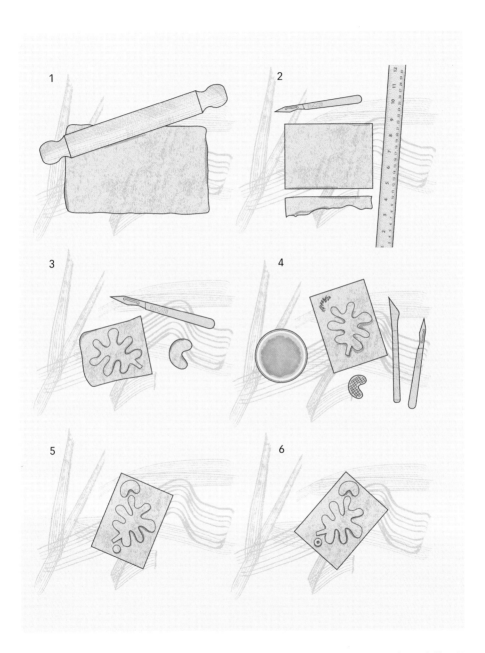

to finish

1 Once your incense holder is dry, sand down any rough patches using a small piece of fine sandpaper.

2 When you are ready to decorate your incense holder, cover your work surface with newspaper or baking paper (parchment) and place the incense holder on it. Pour some black acrylic paint into a small dish and water it down.

3 Dip the bristles of an old toothbrush into the paint, then hold it a few centimetres away from the incense holder and run your finger along the bristles. This will cause the paint to fleck onto your clay. Be careful, this can be very messy! Repeat the process to create as many speckles as you like. Leave to dry for 4 hours.

4 Once the paint is dry, coat your incense holder in a thin layer of clear varnish, using a clean paintbrush. Leave it to dry for another 24 hours before using.

botanical wall hanging

Tools and materials
makes 1

To make:
- 400 g (14 oz) white air-drying clay
- Scales
- Rolling pin
- Scalpel
- Dried flowers
- Skewer or knitting needle

To finish:
- Fine sandpaper
- Your choice of watercolour paints
- Small paintbrush
- Clear water-based varnish
- Paintbrush for varnishing
- 25-cm (10-inch) length of ribbon

Capture the innate beauty of the natural world in all its elegance and complexity with this botanical wall hanging. There are a few ways to approach this project. You can buy your flowers pre-dried or – for a burst of nostalgia – use a flower press to dry your own hand-picked flowers. If you are drying the flowers yourself, you can use a combination of wildflowers, or use shop-bought flowers for an equally beautiful effect.

The thing I love about this project is that it straddles the line between order and chaos. It's so satisfying to make something that is as beautiful and idiosyncratic as nature itself.

to make

1 Cover your work surface, and weigh out 400 g (14 oz) of clay. Roll it into a ball using your hands.

2 With your rolling pin, roll the clay into a rough oval shape measuring approximately 25 x 20 cm (10 x 8 inches).

3 Neaten up the edges of your oval using a sharp scalpel.

4 Place your dried flowers on top of the clay and gently press them into the clay using your hands. Try not to press too hard or you will distort the shape of your wall hanging. To make more of an impact in the clay, gently roll your rolling pin over the top of the dried flowers.

5 Peel off the dried flowers. Don't worry if you end up leaving parts of the flowers behind; you can brush these off once your clay has dried. Neaten up the edges of your wall hanging by dipping your finger into some water and running it around the edge of the piece of clay.

6 Pierce two holes at the top of the wall hanging, using a skewer or knitting needle. The holes need to be large enough for you to thread your ribbon through once the clay is dry. Leave your wall hanging to dry for 24 hours, turning it upside down after 12 hours so that the clay dries evenly.

Spend time in nature, appreciate the beauty.

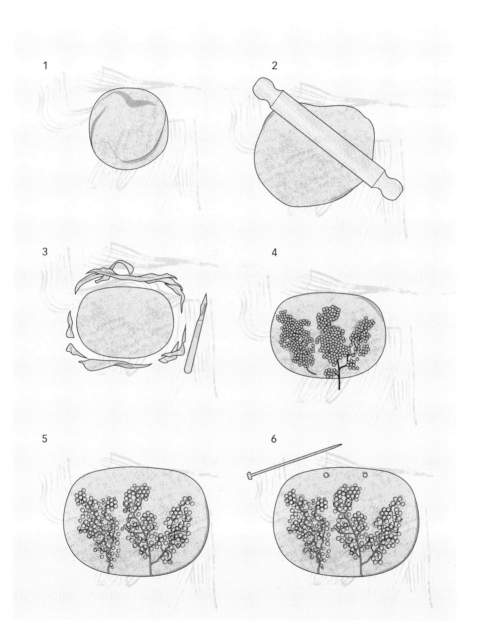

to finish

1 Once your clay has dried, brush off any remaining dried flowers and smooth any rough edges using fine sandpaper. You can either leave your wall hanging plain, with the flower imprints, or you can paint in some of the detail to highlight the pattern of the flowers.

2 If you are painting your wall hanging, water down your chosen watercolour paints and apply to the indents in the clay using a small paintbrush. Leave to dry for 4 hours.

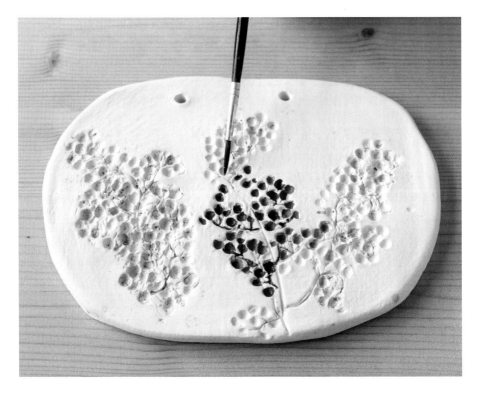

3 Once the paint has dried, you can either leave the wall hanging as it is, or apply a thin coat of clear varnish, using a clean, medium-sized paintbrush, then leave to dry for 24 hours.

4 Once your wall hanging is completely dry, thread your piece of ribbon through one of the holes from the back to the front, then thread it through the other hole from the front to the back.

5 Tie each end of the ribbon in a knot. Your wall hanging is now ready to hang.

bespoke potted
herb markers

Tools and materials
makes 5

To make:
- 500 g (1 lb 2 oz) white air-drying clay
- Scales
- Rolling pin
- Metal ruler
- Scalpel
- Cling film (plastic wrap)
- Alphabet stamps
- Clay modelling tools

To finish:
- Sandpaper
- Acrylic craft paints
- Small dishes (for the paints)
- Thin and medium-sized acrylic paintbrushes
- Clear water-based varnish
- Medium paintbrush for varnishing

Growing your own kitchen herbs is a great way to introduce some colour to your home – it's such a lovely treat to see them all lined up on a sun-soaked windowsill. These herb markers are a useful way to identify what you're grown, because although beautiful, herbs can sometimes look very similar. Imagine confusing your mint with your oregano!

You can really taste the difference when you grow your own herbs, not to mention save money at the same time. It's great to flavour food with something you have grown – we all know it always tastes better when you've grown it yourself.

thyme

to make

1 Cover your work surface, and weigh out 500 g (1 lb 2 oz) of air-drying clay. This will be enough to make five herb markers. Roll out your clay so that it measures roughly 20 x 20 cm (8 x 8 inches) and is 1 cm (½ inch) thick all over.

2 With your ruler, measure out five triangles, 13 cm (5 inches) high and 6 cm (2½ inches) wide at their base. Cut out the triangles using your ruler and a sharp scalpel. Wrap the excess clay up in some cling film (plastic wrap), but keep one piece aside for use in step 4.

3 Clean up any rough edges on your triangles using a dab of water and your finger.

4 Before you start making any marks on your triangles with your alphabet stamps or clay modelling tools, practise on a spare piece of clay. This way you will know how much pressure to apply while using the stamps, and you can also experiment with the different patterns each modelling tool makes.

5 When you are confident to start decorating your triangles, begin by pressing the alphabet stamps into the clay to form the name of each herb. Make sure the stamps are clean before you start using them. You will need to apply medium pressure to achieve enough depth for the letters to be readable.

6 Add some more decoration and patterns using your clay modelling tools. Once you have finished, leave your markers to dry for 24 hours, turning them over after 12 hours so that the clay dries evenly.

Notice the texture in the clay, the patterns your hands make, the beauty.

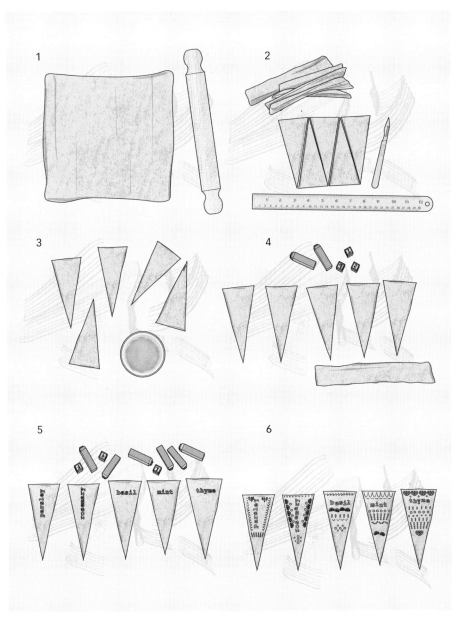

1

2

3

4

5

parsley rosemary basil mint thyme

6

parsley rosemary basil mint thyme

to finish

1 Once your markers are dry, smooth any rough edges using fine sandpaper.

2 Prepare your paints. Pour a small amount of each of your chosen colours into small dishes and water them down a little to create a 'wash'.

3 To bring out the name of the herb, use a thin paintbrush to carefully apply a dark 'wash' to each of the letters and indents on your markers. Leave to dry for 4 hours.

4 Once the paint is completely dry, coat one side of the markers in a layer of clear varnish, using a medium-sized clean paintbrush. Wait 24 hours for this to dry before turning over and coating the other side. Leave to dry for another 24 hours before adding the markers to your plant pots.

foraged leaf dish

Tools and materials
makes 1

To make:
- 200 g (7 oz) white air-drying clay
- Scales
- Rolling pin
- Leaf, approximately 13 x 13 cm (5 x 5 inches)
- Scalpel
- Cling film (plastic wrap)
- Bowl or mold, at least 15 cm (6 inches) in diameter

To make:
- Fine sandpaper
- Acrylic craft paints
- Small dishes (for the paints)
- Thin and medium acrylic paintbrushes
- Clear water-based varnish
- Medium paintbrush for varnishing

This one-of-a-kind trinket dish is a quick and easy way to spruce up your bedside table, and makes a fun craft activity for all ages. It's a perfect project for children during long school holidays, especially on rainy days – take a trip down to your nearest woodland and have a rummage for the perfect leaf! Combining nature and craft is bound to entertain small hands.

If you enjoy making this dish, consider creating a variety of dishes using different-shaped leaves.

to make

1 Cover your work surface, and weigh out 200 g (7 oz) of white air-drying clay. Roll out your clay so that it is 5 mm (¼ inch) thick all over and 20 x 15 cm (8 x 6 inches) in size – large enough for a leaf that is approximately 13 x 13 cm (5 x 5 inches).

2 Place your clean, dry leaf face down on your clay. Roll your rolling pin over the leaf a few times, applying medium pressure so that the leaf sticks to the clay.

3 Using a scalpel, cut around the leaf, leaving a 0.5–1-cm (¼–½-inch) border of clay all the way around.

4 Smooth any rough edges of the clay with your finger and a dab of water.

5 Place a piece of cling film (plastic wrap) inside your bowl or mold. This will stop your clay from sticking to the bowl while it dries. Gently press your clay leaf shape into the bottom of the bowl. This will give your leaf dish its curved shape. Leave to dry for 24 hours.

6 Once the clay leaf is dry, gently remove it from the bowl and peel off the leaf to reveal the pattern underneath.

Take a moment to stop.

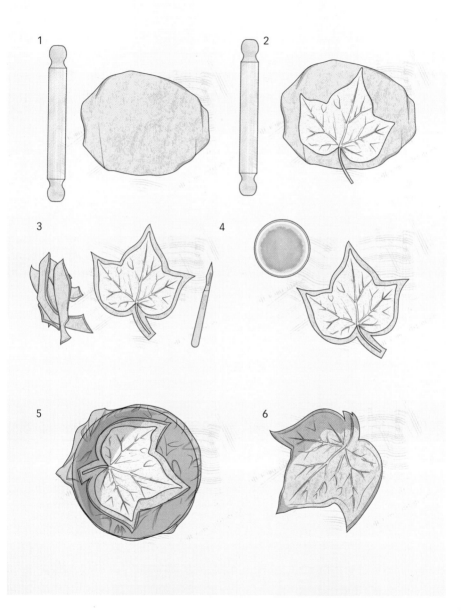

1

2

3

4

5

6

to finish

1 You can either leave your leaf dish plain or add some detail to the marks that were left behind by the leaf. Before you apply any paint, smooth any rough edges using fine sandpaper.

2 Prepare your acrylic paint. Pour a small amount into a small dish and water it down a little.

3 Use a medium paintbrush to apply a layer of paint within the border of the leaf. When the background is dry to the touch, apply details along the veins of the leaf using a thin paintbrush. You can add as little or as much detail as you like. Leave to dry for 4 hours.

4 Once the paint is dry, apply a layer of varnish to the top of your dish, using a medium-sized clean paintbrush. Leave to dry for 24 hours, then turn over and coat the bottom of the dish. Leave to dry for another 24 hours.

boho plant hanger

Tools and materials
makes 1

To make:
- 450 g (1 lb) terracotta air-drying clay
- Scales
- Rolling pin
- Circular 8.5-cm (3½-inch) cookie cutter
- Metal ruler
- Scalpel
- Clay modelling tools
- Thin knitting needle or skewer

To finish:
- Fine sandpaper
- White acrylic craft paint
- Small dish (for the paint)
- Pencil with rubber on the end
- Clear water-based varnish
- Medium paintbrush for varnishing
- 3 m (10 feet) of cord or thin rope
- 1 x 6-cm (2½-inch) wooden ring

Bring back the 1970s with this bohemian-inspired plant hanger. The terracotta clay can be left plain or spruced up with some simple jazzy patterns, while the simple knotted ropes are ideal if you love the look of macramé but feel that the elaborate knots might be a little too complicated for your liking.

Once you've made the plant hanger, pop a plant inside and admire your spruced-up plant corner.

You'll be surprised how much of a difference a bit more greenery will make to your day-to-day living space.

to make

1 First, cover your work surface, then roll out the terracotta air-drying clay out into a long rectangle shape measuring approximately 40 x 9 cm (16 x 3½ inches). The clay needs to be roughly 5 mm (¼ inch) thick.

2 Cut out a circle at one end of the clay, using your 8.5-cm (3½-inch) cookie cutter.

3 With the remaining clay, measure and cut out a rectangle measuring 30 x 9 cm (12 x 3½ inches).

4 The circle of clay will form the base of your pot. To assemble your pot, wrap the long rectangle of clay around the edge of the circle, gently pressing the clay together. The two ends of the rectangle will overlap; use your fingers to gently smooth the edges together, but try not to press too hard or you will lose the shape of the pot.

5 You now need to secure the join between the base and the sides of the pot. Take a small coin-size piece of clay between your hands and roll it to form a worm shape 8 cm (3 inches) long. Place this inside the pot at the join, and push down gently using your clay tool. Repeat until the entire join is covered and secure. When this dries, it will create the glue to hold the two pieces together.

6 To create the holes for the rope, take your knitting needle or skewer and pierce four evenly spaced holes in the sides of the pot, near the top. Leave your pot to dry for 24 hours, turning it upside down halfway through the drying time so that it dries evenly.

Create a calm space to make in, sit comfortably.

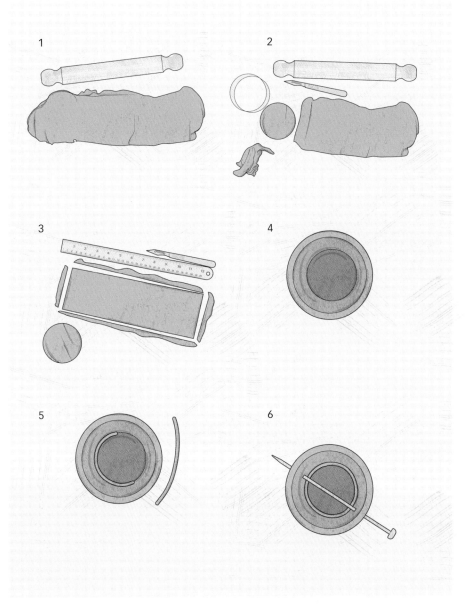

1

2

3

4

5

6

to finish

1 Once your pot is dry, sand down any rough edges. You can either leave your pot plain and varnish it, or add some decoration, as shown.

2 Pour the white acrylic paint into a small dish. Dip the rubber end of a pencil into the paint and dab it onto your pot. You can either create a geometric pattern or dot randomly around the pot. Leave to dry for 4 hours.

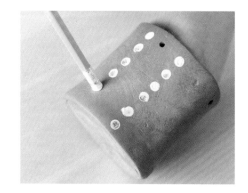

3 Once the paint is dry, coat the pot with a layer of clear varnish, inside and out, and leave to dry for 24 hours.

4 Cut a piece of cord measuring 1.5 m (5 feet). Thread one end through one of the holes in your pot, tying a knot on the inside. Thread the other end of the cord first through the wooden ring and then through the hole on the opposite side of the pot, again tying a knot on the inside.

5 Repeat step 4 with another 1.5 m (5 feet) length of rope, threading it through the other two holes in your pot.

6 Pull the wooden ring up and bring all the ropes together. Your planter is now ready to hang.

minimalist indoor planter

Tools and materials
makes 1

To make:
- 1kg (2 lb 3 oz) white air-drying clay
- Scales
- Rolling pin
- Metal ruler
- Scalpel
- Cling film (plastic wrap)
- Clay modelling tools

To finish:
- Fine sandpaper
- Acrylic craft paints
- Small dishes (for the paints)
- Thin and medium acrylic paintbrushes
- Clear water-based varnish
- Medium paintbrush for varnishing

Plants don't just brighten up a room – they can improve your focus and mood, and help purify the air, too. That's why I believe there's no reason not to fill your home with them!

This lovely little planter makes the perfect home for a row of air plant babies. Leave it simple for a modern, clean Scandinavian look, or decorate it with craft paints to add your own unique touch. Either way, enjoy looking after your plants – it's said that talking to them helps them grow!

The clay is not watertight, so take the plants out to spray them.

to make

1 Cover your work surface. You will make the planter first, and then the stand. To make the planter, weigh out 750 g (1 lb 10 oz) of white air-drying clay, and wrap the remainder in cling film (plastic wrap) so that it doesn't dry out.

2 Roll out the clay so that it measures approximately 30 x 25 cm (12 x 10 inches) and is around 5 mm (¼ inch) thick all over.

3 Use a ruler to measure out the five pieces that will be used to make your planter. The base needs to be 19 x 8 cm (7½ x 3 inches); the two longer sides are 19 x 5 cm (7½ x 2 inches); and the two shorter sides are 8 x 5 cm (3 x 2 inches). Cut out the pieces using a ruler and a scalpel. Wrap the leftover clay trimmings in cling film (plastic wrap), to be used later.

4 Now attach the sides of the planter to the base. First, take one of the clay scraps left over from step 3 and roll it into a long, thin snake shape. Holding one of the side pieces next to the base, place the snake-shaped piece of clay in the join. Using a clay modelling tool, gently press and merge the snake-shaped clay piece into the clay base and side of the planter. Use your other hand to support the 'wall' of the planter as you are doing this.

5 Repeat step 4 to attach the other three sides of your planter. Once it is assembled, smooth out any rough edges with your finger and a dab of water. Leave the planter to one side.

6 You will now make the stand for the planter. Roll out the remaining 250 g (9 oz) of white air-drying clay so that it measures 20 x 10 cm (8 x 4 inches) and is around 5 mm (¼ inch) thick all over.

Take your mind to a calm, centred place and squeeze the clay between your fingers.

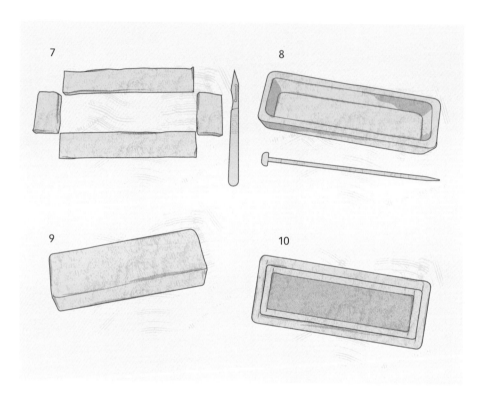

7 Measure and cut out four pieces of clay using a ruler and a scalpel: you need two pieces measuring 16 x 2.5 cm (6½ x 1 inches) and two pieces measuring 5 x 2.5 cm (2 x 1 inches).

8 Join the four pieces of the stand together, one at a time, by merging snake-shaped pieces of clay into the joins, as you did with the planter. Smooth out any rough edges using a dab of water and your finger.

9 Leave both the planter and the stand to dry for 24 hours. Turn the planter upside down after 12 hours to allow its base to dry.

10 When the planter and stand are dry, they can be joined together. Turn the planter upside down and centre the stand on top of it. Using some of the scraps of clay you set aside in step 3, roll out some snake-shaped clay pieces and place them around the inside of the stand, where it joins the planter base. Use a clay modelling tool to gently merge the snake-shaped pieces onto the sides of the stand and the base of the planter. Leave to dry for 24 hours.

to finish

1 Once your planter is assembled and completely dry, smooth any rough edges with some fine sandpaper. You can either leave your planter plain and varnish it, or add some decoration, as shown.

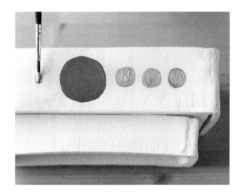

2 If you are painting your planter, apply your design using acrylic paint and a medium and thin paintbrush. Paint on any shapes you like. You can mark where you want to place the shapes with a pencil. Make sure you start with the lighter colours; darker colours should be applied last. Leave to dry for 24 hours.

3 Once it is dry, apply a layer of clear varnish to the inside and outside of your planter, using a clean, medium-sized paintbrush, and leave to dry for 24 hours. Turn over and coat the base, then leave to dry for another 24 hours.

botanical festive decorations

Tools and materials
makes 8

To make:
- 500 g (1 lb 2 oz) white air-drying clay
- Scales
- Rolling pin
- Clay modelling tools
- Thin knitting needle or skewer
- Circular 6.5-cm (2½-inch) cookie cutter
- Scalpel

To finish:
- Fine sandpaper
- Gold acrylic paint
- Small dish (for the paint)
- Thin acrylic paintbrush
- Thin blue paint pen, with a line width of 1.8–2.5 mm
- Clear water-based varnish
- Paintbrush for varnishing
- 160-cm (64-inch) length of gold string
- Washi or masking tape

The festive period can be a little overwhelming. If you are feeling the strain, take a step back from the hubbub and set aside some time for yourself to make these beautiful decorations, which draw inspiration from the calming influence of nature and allow you to add a personal touch to the festivities.

The non-traditional blue-and-gold colour palette may feel bold, but experimentation is its own reward and will make your decorations authentically 'you'. The metallic gold paint will give your decorations a subtle festive lustre.

This project makes eight decorations, enough to hang some on your own tree and to give some away. Tie them to your wrapped gifts for that extra-special touch – the very best present you can give is a bit of yourself.

Admire your work, feel pleasure at a job well done.

to make

1 First, cover your work surface. To make eight decorations, you will need to weigh out 500 g (1 lb 2 oz) of white air-drying clay.

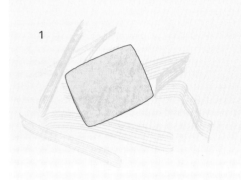

2 Begin by making the larger beads. Using one of your clay modelling tools, cut eight small cubes of clay measuring roughly 2 cm (¾ inch), and roll them into balls using your hands. Try to smooth out any cracks at this stage.

3 Pierce a hole through each bead, using a thin knitting needle or skewer. This will allow you to thread the decorations later.

4 Repeat steps 2 and 3 to create another eight beads, but this time use slightly smaller cubes of clay, roughly 1 cm (½ inch) big, and squash the balls between your fingers to create smaller, flatter beads. You should now have 16 beads.

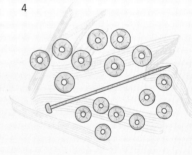

5 Next, make the discs for your decorations. Roll out the rest of the clay, keeping it 5 mm (¼ inch) thick all over.

6 Cut out four circular shapes using your cookie cutter. If you don't have a cookie cutter, you can lightly draw around the bottom of a glass using a scalpel, and cut out the shape.

7 Pierce a hole at the top of each disc, using a knitting needle or skewer. The hole needs to be big enough for the cord to fit through later, when the decorations are threaded. Dip your finger in water and gently run it around the edges of the discs, to smooth any rough edges.

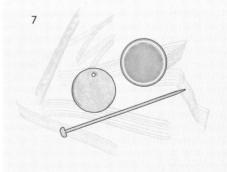

8 Now make four oval-shaped discs. Use your scalpel to draw freehand four long oval shapes, and cut them out. Then repeat steps 7 and 8 to make holes in your discs and smooth the rough edges.

9 Once you have made all your pieces for your decorations, leave them to dry for 24 hours. Turn the discs over halfway through, so that they dry evenly.

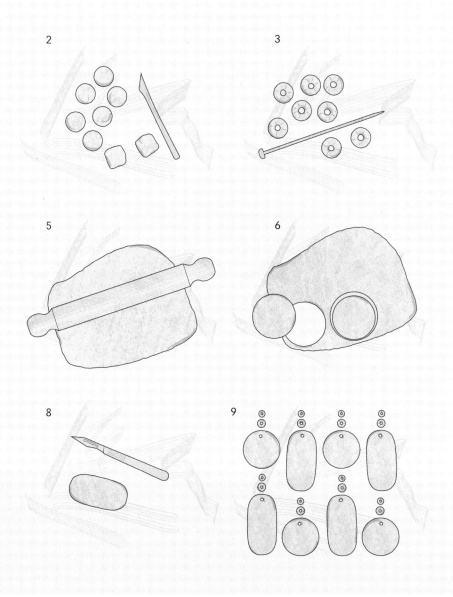

to finish

1 Once your decorations are dry, sand off any rough edges using fine sandpaper.

2 Pour the gold acrylic paint into a small dish. Paint eight of the beads, covering them completely. If you place the beads on the end of a paintbrush or skewer before painting, this will help to give a nice, even coating and minimize mess.

3 Paint small vertical gold dashes around the circumferences of the remaining eight beads. Put all the beads to one side and leave to dry for 4 hours.

4 Next draw the botanical illustrations on the eight discs, using a thin blue paint pen. You can either copy the illustrations shown or draw your own design; practise your designs on a sheet of paper first if you like. The paint pen will give you more control over your lines than a paintbrush, and will result in neater flowers. Leave the discs to dry for 4 hours.

5 Once the beads and discs are dry, coat them in a layer of clear varnish, using a clean paintbrush, and leave to dry for 24 hours. You will need to coat the discs with varnish one side at a time.

6 Once your decorations are dry and ready to assemble, cut eight pieces of gold cord, each around 20 cm (8 inches) long. Take a disc and thread a length of cord through it, then wrap the two ends together with a piece of washi or masking tape and make a sharp point. This makes it easier to thread the beads. Thread the wrapped cord end first through the larger bead and then through the flatter bead. Tie the cord at the top and snip off the tape. Repeat for the other seven decorations.

ditzy miniature bunting

Tools and materials

makes approximately 40 bunting flags

To make:
- 500g (1 lb 2 oz) white air-drying clay
- Scales
- Rolling pin
- Metal ruler
- Scalpel
- Thin knitting needle or skewer

To finish:
- Sandpaper
- Scraps of thin quilting fabric in different colours
- Fabric scissors
- Craft glue
- Small paintbrush for gluing
- 3 m (10 feet) of gold wire, 0.5 mm thick
- 6 wooden beads

Bunting is cheerful and uplifting by its very nature! The bunting you can buy in shops is generally made from fabric or knitted into perfect little triangles, but you won't find anything quite like this delicate miniature clay bunting, which will bring a truly personal touch to your home. You can keep it simple and chic by leaving it plain, or embellish it with pretty flowery fabric.

Bunting isn't just for the street parties these days – it will look lovely in any room, whether you are putting it up for a special occasion or adding some colour and flair to your everyday decor.

to make

1 First, cover your work surface. Weigh out 500 g (1 lb 2 oz) of air-drying clay and roll out the clay until it is roughly 5 cm (2 inches) thick all over. The piece of rolled-out clay should measure roughly 30 x 25 cm (12 x 10 inches).

2 Measure and then cut your clay into five horizontal strips, using your ruler and scalpel. Each strip should be 5 cm (2 inches) in height.

3 Cut each strip into triangles.

4 You will need approximately 40 triangles, but don't worry if you have more or less.

5 With a thin knitting needle or skewer, make holes in two of the corners of each triangle. The holes need to be big enough for the gold wire to fit through later, when the bunting is threaded.

6 Smooth any rough edges with a dab of water and your finger, then leave the triangles to dry for 24 hours.

Live life one day at a time.

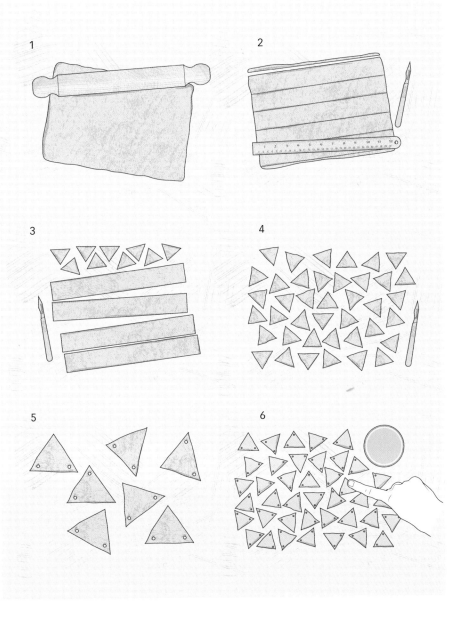

1

2

3

4

5

6

to finish

1　If your triangles have any rough edges once they are dry, spend a little time sanding them with a small piece of sandpaper.

2　You can either keep your triangles plain and simple, or you can add flowery fabric shapes to make them completely unique. To do this, cut out small traingles of fabric in various sizes and colours.

3　Apply a layer of glue to the clay triangle, place the fabric triangle on top, then cover the fabric with a layer of glue. Leave the triangles to dry completely for 4 hours.

4 Once the glue is completely dry, your bunting is ready to assemble. Cut a long piece of gold wire, then thread the triangles onto it one at a time, passing the wire through one hole and then back out of the other. Thread a ready-made wooden bead onto the wire after every 6 triangles. This will add a lovely rustic touch.

5 Bend the wire into a loop and twist it around itself to create a loop. Trim off any excess. Your bunting is now ready to be hung on a hook or nail on the wall.

feather wall hanging

Tools and materials
makes 14 feathers

To make:
- 250 g (9 oz) white air-drying clay
- Cling film (plastic wrap)
- Scales
- Rolling pin
- Scalpel
- Clay modelling tools
- Scissors

To finish:
- Fine sandpaper
- Acrylic gold paint
- Small dish (for the paint)
- Small flat acrylic paintbrush
- Clear water-based varnish
- Paintbrush for varnishing
- 4 m (13 feet) of gold wire, 0.5 mm thick
- 30-cm (12-inch) length of wooden dowel or piece of driftwood, 1 cm (½ inch) in diameter

Have you ever wanted to add a little bohemian touch to your living room wall but didn't know where to start? This feathery wall hanging will look lovely in any household and is a real delight to make. The delicate handmade feathers are really beautiful; don't worry about them being perfect – your feathers will be slightly different shapes and sizes, but this is what will make your wall hanging so unique. Just enjoy the calming, mindful process of making them.

If the gold decoration is not for you, or if it doesn't go with your room's colour scheme, you can use an alternative colour to match your home decor or leave the feathers plain for a serene, minimal look.

Appreciate the moment.

to make

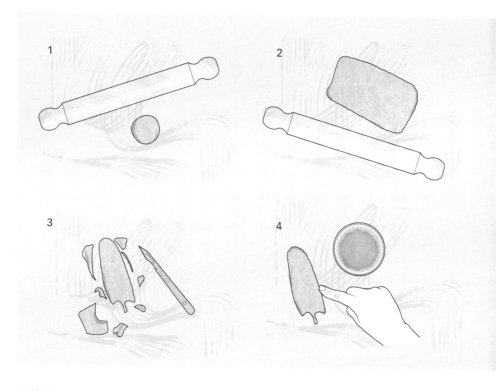

1 First, cover your work surface. Break off a small piece of clay and roll it into a small ball, about the size of a golf ball. Wrap the rest of the clay in cling film (plastic wrap) to protect it from drying out and put it to one side.

2 Using your rolling pin, roll the ball of clay out to approximately 3 mm (⅛ inch) thick all over.

3 Using the scalpel, lightly draw the outline of a feather, approximately 4 cm (1½ inches) wide and 12 cm (4½ inches) tall, and then carefully cut it out. Don't worry about the feather being perfect; you will want them to vary slightly in size and shape.

4 Dip your finger into some water and gently run it around the edges of the feather, to smooth any rough edges.

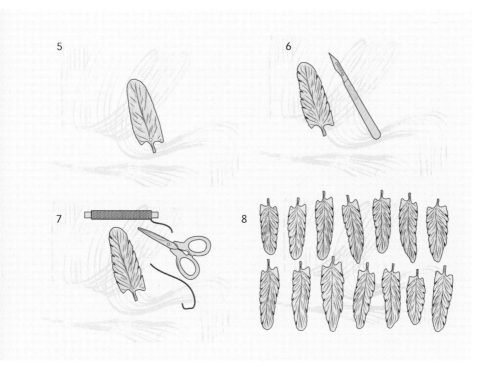

5 Once you are happy with your feather shape, you are ready to add detail. Using the sharp edge of your modelling tool, draw a long line running down the centre of the feather, from the 'quill' to the tip. For a more realistic look, draw a line with a slight curve. Then, working your way from top to bottom to avoid smudging, draw short, slanted strokes from the centre of the feather to both edges.

6 To add more detail to your feather, cut into the edges with your scalpel every 1 cm (½ inch). Use your fingers to lift the edges to create some texture and a sense of movement in your feather.

7 Using a thin piece of wire, poke a small hole through the clay at the point where the 'quill' joins the body of the feather, making sure it's not too close to the edge. The hole needs to be big enough for the wire to fit through later, when the feathers are threaded.

8 Using the clay that you put aside in step 1, repeat steps 1–7 until you have 14 clay feathers – 12 for the wall hanging and two spares in case of breakages. Put the feathers to one side and leave to dry for 24 hours.

to finish

1 Once your feathers are dry, sand off any rough
edges using fine sandpaper. Be extra careful
while doing this, as your clay feathers are
extremely thin and fragile.

2 You can either leave your feathers plain or paint
them before varnishing. If you are painting them,
coat the ends of the feathers, varying the length of
the paint, either 5 cm (2 inches) or 2 cm (¾ inch).

3 Leave the feathers to dry for 4 hours by placing them on the edge of a table or on a raised surface, like a piece of wood, with the painted edges hanging over the edge.

4 Once your feathers are dry, apply a layer of clear varnish to one side, using a clean paintbrush. Leave to dry for 12 hours, then turn the feathers over and paint the other side with varnish. Leave to dry for 12 hours.

5 Once the feathers are completely dry, cut 12 pieces of gold wire of varying lengths, from 20 cm (8 inches) to 30 cm (12 inches). Take a feather and thread a piece of wire about 3 cm (1 inch) through the hole. Bend the wire back and twist it around the longer end of the wire a few times to secure. Repeat for the other 11 feathers.

6 Attach the feathers to your wooden dowel (or driftwood) one at a time, by wrapping the ends of the wires around the dowel a few times and then twisting the wire around itself to secure. Trim any excess wire or simply wrap it around the dowel.

7 Space the feathers unevenly along the dowel, to create little clusters of feathers. Start in the middle and work your way out.

8 Cut a piece of gold wire approximately 50 cm (20 inches) in length. Attach the wire to the dowel around 2 cm (¾ inch) from the end, by wrapping it around the dowel a few times and then twisting the wire around itself to secure. Repeat with the other end of the wire at the opposite end of the dowel. Your hanging is now ready to be secured safely to the wall.

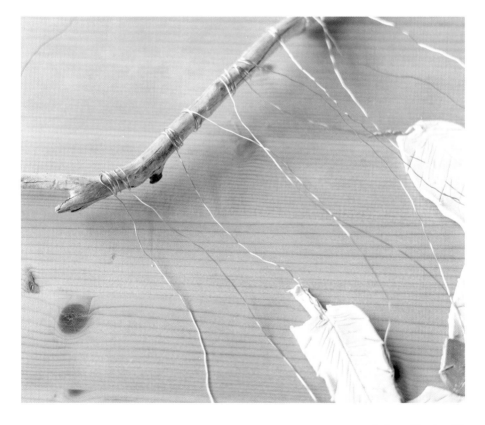

nature-inspired serving dishes

Tools and materials
makes 1

To make:
- 1 small dish, approx. 22 x 12 cm (9¾ x 5¾ inches)
- Cling film (plastic wrap)
- 250g white air-drying clay
- Scales
- Rolling pin
- Scalpel

To finish:
- Fine sandpaper
- Pencil (optional)
- Acrylic craft paints
- Small dishes (for the paints)
- Acrylic paintbrushes, various sizes
- Clear water-based varnish
- Large paintbrush for varnishing

Have you got any old, unloved serving dishes or plates at the back of the cupboard? If you like their shape and style but aren't so sure about the pattern, this project allows you to make your own, unique version of them, using the dishes as a base for the shape but giving you a creative free rein on the design.

The nature-inspired design suggested for this dish uses repeated flower and fruit patterns. The process of painting the patterns is truly calming and can send you off into a meditative state, perfect for those days when you just want to sit quietly with your thoughts. This is also a great project to do with children, as the techniques used are so straightforward. Let your little ones loose with the paints and see what they come up with, then bloom with pride next time you serve the nibbles at a party.

to make

1 To protect your serving dish and prevent the air-drying clay from sticking to it, cover it completely in cling film (plastic wrap). Make sure the cling film is slightly loose, so that you can push it into any grooves.

2 Cover your work surface. To make the first dish, weigh out 250 g (9 oz) of air-drying clay and roll it out so that it is approximately 5 mm (¼ inch) thick. The rolled-out clay should be big enough so that, when it is placed on top of your dish, there is roughly 3 cm (1 inch) of spare clay around the edge.

3 Place the rolled-out piece of clay over the top of your dish and use your fingers to gently push it down into the corners, so that it forms the shape of the dish. You will need to use both hands for this step – one for holding the clay, and the other for shaping.

4 Once you are happy with the shape, carefully trim off the excess clay by gently skimming a scalpel alongside the edge of the dish.

5 Smooth out any rough edges with your finger and a dab of water. Leave to dry for 24 hours.

6 Now you've got the hang of it, get some more clay and try steps 1–5 with other shaped dishes.

Sit with nature, listen to the birds, breathe.

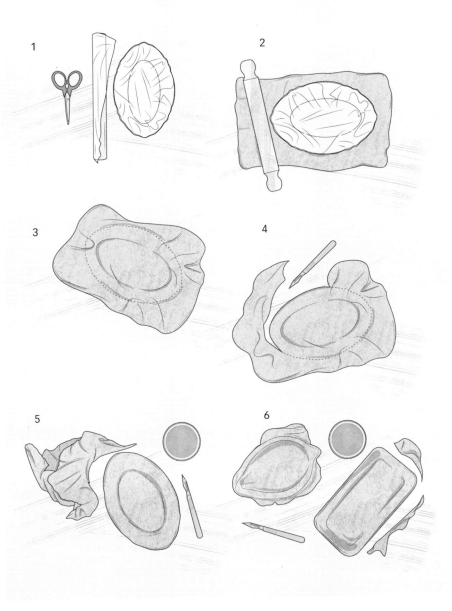

to finish

1 Once your dish is dry, release the cling film (plastic wrap) from the original dish. Your clay dish should easily lift off.

2 If there are any rough edges, sand them down before painting.

3 Your dish can now be decorated. If you are not confident about starting to paint straight away, draw out your design with a pencil beforehand.

4 Paint in your fruit or flower designs, using acrylic craft paints and various sized paintbrushes. Start with your base colour, then wait until the background is dry to the touch.

5 Paint in the other details. Leave your painted dish to dry for 4 hours.

6 Once the paint is dry, use a clean paintbrush to coat your dish with a clear varnish and leave to dry for 24 hours. Remember that this clay is not waterproof, so your dish should be wiped clean after use, not washed. If you are using the dish for food, place a napkin down beforehand to prevent oil and grease from soaking into the clay.

precious seaside vase

Tools and materials
makes 1

To make:
- Old vase
- Terracotta air-drying clay: 1.6 kg (3 lb 10 oz) of clay will cover a vase 18 cm (7 inches) high and 16 cm (6¼ inches) in diameter
- Scales

To finish:
- Shells in various shapes and sizes

If you are lucky enough to live by the sea, you can't help but be inspired by it. There is no better way to clear your head than a slow, mindful meander along the shore, aimlessly seeking out any pretty shells you can find. This upcycled seaside vase makes use of any pearly treasures you might have collected that have ended up sitting on a shelf collecting dust.

The project is simple, so anyone can have a go at it. There's no need to be overly perfect with the clay – the rougher the better. You can use any shaped vase or pot you might have lying around, or pick one up from your local second-hand shop. We have used terracotta air-drying clay, but for a cleaner, more modern feel, the vase also looks great made with white air-drying clay.

Because the original pot remains in place underneath the clay covering, the vase can still be filled with water and used to hold flowers.

Making is a form of meditation. Meditate on the things you appreciate in life.

to make

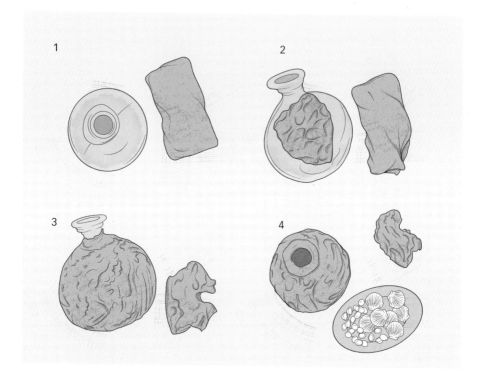

1 Clean your vase with warm, soapy water and leave to dry. When it is completely dry, cover your work surface and weigh out your clay.

2 Begin to cover your vase by taking small handfuls of clay and flattening it down onto the vase with your fingertips.

3 Work your way around the vase, placing more and more handfuls of clay. Work as quickly as you can to avoid the clay setting. Don't worry about smoothing out all the lines and finger marks, as they will be covered later if you are adding shells. The clay should be about 1.5 cm (⅝ inch) thick all the way around.

4 Repeat this process until your vase is completely covered around the sides and rim. Leave the base and inside of the vase free from clay – this way you will be able to put water inside it and use it for fresh flowers. You could at this point leave your pot to dry for 3 days and then sand and paint it, or you can decorate it with the shells you've collected. If you are decorating it with shells, you will need to do this straight away while the clay is still 'wet' and moldable (see opposite).

to finish

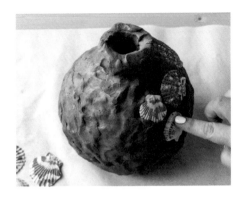

1. With clean hands, start placing your shells on the clay vase, pushing them down into the clay. Make sure your shells are nice and secure; you will notice the clay gripping the edges of the shells.

2. Work your way around your vase, alternating between large and small shells. Fill in any blank sections with smaller shells. You can either create a pattern with the shells or make the decoration more random, as on the vase shown here.

3. Once you have finished decorating your vase with the shells, leave it to dry for 3 days. Make sure the clay is completely dry before you fill the vase with water.

Author Biography

Lucy Davidson is a contemporary crafter and designer who specializes in pottery and weaving as Peas & Needles. She teaches workshops and classes, and has featured in the national press with her original step-by-step projects and techniques for the modern maker to create at home. Lucy blogs about making, craft & design, and has appeared on Channel 4 television in the UK. www.peasandneedles.co.uk/Insta_ peasandneedles.